PRAYING WITH ANOTHER FOR HEALING

Dennis Linn, Matthew Linn, and Sheila Fabricant

Paulist Press
New York/Ramsey

Library of Congress
Catalog Card Number: 83-62947

ISBN: 0-8091-2619-2

Published by *Paulist Press*
545 Island Road, Ramsey, N.J. 07446

Printed and bound in the
United States of America

Contents

Dedicated to

Agnes Sanford and Francis MacNutt *in gratitude*
for teaching us how to pray with Jesus' healing love

Book Map—How to
Use this Book

This book can be used in three ways:

1. As a book offering information for improving your prayer alone or with another. Simply read Part I.

2. As a seminar used alone, with another, or with a group. Read a chapter in Part I. Then during the week do the prayer and journaling exercises in the corresponding seminar session in Part II. For fuller seminar teaching consult Appendix E for *Praying with Another for Healing* video tape (also rented on a donation basis) and audio tape purchase.

3. Any way you want.

PART I: PRAYER WITH ANOTHER FOR HEALING

Introduction:
Why Pray with Another

When we think of Jesus praying, we often think of the "Lord's Prayer" or of Jesus going off alone to a quiet place. But Jesus probably spent most of his prayer time praying with another person for healing. Why did he spend so much time praying with another for healing?

I believe Jesus prayed constantly with others for healing not to prove he was God but simply because Jesus was God. As God, he could not just proclaim the Father's compassion in words but he had to pray compassionately with others even when the laws forbade curing a withered hand on the sabbath or touching to heal the unclean leper (Lev 13:11; Mt 8:4; Mk 3:1–6). Because he was so full of the Father's compassion, Jesus, unlike the prophets who never called others to heal, called every believer to follow him in laying hands upon the afflicted and praying for healing (Mk 16:18). In praying for healing with the afflicted, we and all believers touch the suffering in another and carry it in our hearts to the Father's heart. Jesus knew that this was the easiest way for us to learn and experience the Father's healing, compassionate love.

Everyone who has met the Father's love and can stand in that beside another who is suffering can pray simply and powerfully for healing. Sr. Gloriana Bednarski works in midtown Chicago in a halfway house for the mentally ill who suffer from depression or schizophrenia and cannot cope with ordinary life. Because she too once suffered mental illness, she has a heart filled with compassion and trust in the Father's healing love. Sr. Gloriana teaches the patients how to place their hands gently on the shoulders of a depressed patient while saying: "Jesus within me wants to give you his peace. Just take a few deep breaths and breathe in his peace now." Usually the depressed patient can begin to breathe in the peace that is in the other's heart. Before Sr. Gloriana taught the patients to do this, many had to be sent away and treated at the Elgin hospital for severe depression. In the years since she has taught her patients to lay hands on one another, none have had to be sent away.

Not only patients in a mental hospital but also professionals are discovering the power in praying with another. For instance, most of the two thousand members of the Association of Christian Therapists find that praying with others in their professional practices has not only added depth to their therapy but also has cut by about a third the time they need to spend with a patient.[1] Such groups as David Wilkerson's Teen Challenge with its stress on healing prayer and Christian community, had higher success rates with drug addicts (77%) than the best New York State program (29%). Priests find more healing happening through the new rite of the sacrament of reconciliation which encourages the laying on of hands and praying with the penitent for healing. Penitents no longer return each week with the same list of sins.[2] Spiritual directors and retreat directors also find that praying with their directees can bring breakthroughs that could otherwise have taken years.[3]

Although all of us from mental patients to retreat directors are empowered to pray for another, the more love we have for another, the more powerful is our prayer. Parents especially have great power to pray for their children. One couple found themselves in heated arguments during an inconvenient pregnancy. Their daughter Joan was born irritable and deaf. Five years later the parents discovered Jesus and allowed him to heal their marriage and the past hurts they carried into their marriage. They then wanted to share Jesus' healing love with their five-year-old deaf daughter, so they decided to pray by laying their hands upon Joan while she slept each night. They simply prayed, "Jesus, be the healing bridge between the love Joan received and the love she needed." They would then tell Jesus and Joan how much they loved her. Slowly Joan lost her irritability, and as they continued this prayer for ninety nights, her ears again opened to take in all of Jesus' healing love.

1. Association of Christian Therapists, 3700 East Ave., Rochester, N.Y. 14618.
2. Michael Scanlon, *The Power in Penance* (Notre Dame: Ave Maria, 1972).
3. Francis A. Sullivan and Robert Faricy, "On Making the Spiritual Exercises for the Renewal of Jesuit Charisms," *Studies in Spirituality of Jesuits* XV: 2 (March 1983), pp. 13-14.

It is easy to pray with children not only when they are asleep but also when they are awake because children usually have an active imagination open to Jesus. A friend of ours noticed that since age three her son Manuel had been afraid of being left alone in a room or any other place such as a car where the doors might close. He was afraid that the door would close and lock, leaving him unable to get out. Yet Manuel couldn't recall ever being locked in a room. But his sister finally remembered that three years before she had been stuck in an elevator while her three-year-old brother panicked. So Manuel's mother sat down with him and had him draw an elevator with himself inside. Manuel drew the elevator buttons way above his reach. Then while she prayed, she had him close his eyes, imagine the elevator, feel his panic and then see Jesus standing next to him. He could see it all and experienced Jesus lifting him up to reach the elevator buttons he couldn't reach. Jesus told him that he was soon going to be big enough to do it all alone, and he never had to worry about getting locked in. All his fear evaporated and he drew a tall Jesus in the picture totally in control. Since that prayer he had no more fear of elevators, being locked in, etc. Two years later he was locked alone in the school gym for two hours and had no fear. Manuel told his mother, "I just closed my eyes and saw Jesus standing next to me. I knew I would be O.K."

Even though so much healing can happen when we too begin to pray lovingly for another, it is still difficult to begin. I (Dennis) resisted praying for healing when I gave a thirty-day retreat to a religious sister with genetic neural damage in her ears. She had to lip-read what I said. I thought, "Maybe if I pray with her, God will restore her hearing." But I didn't have much confidence in my prayers for physical healing because some people I had prayed for recently had died. At that time I didn't understand that death and a resurrected body could be a complete answer to my prayer for healing. So I was discouraged and I thought that if someone else prayed with her, or if she went to a special place, she might be healed. About a year later I received a phone call from this sister. Some members of her community had prayed with her for healing. Even though she still had genetic neural damage, doctors confirmed that her hearing had been totally restored. The doctors were astounded and so was I. I felt both happy and sad. I was happy that she could hear and sad that I had not reached out to pray with her myself. I had tied God's loving hands with my fears.

Just as fear stops me from loving, love stops me from fearing. Although I (Matt) knew that I should pray

with another, I never did it until one I loved much was ill. I had spent the summer living on the Sioux reservation with Mary, a Sioux grandmother, who in teaching me Lakota and the Sioux ways became as close to me as my own grandmother. After I returned to the reservation to teach in the fall, her family asked me to pray with her in the hospital where she was in a coma. I prayed *for* her at Mass and then went to visit her—not to pray *with* her, because that I had never done and feared to do. The nurse told me that Mary's vital signs were failing fast after two weeks in a coma.

When I entered Mary's hospital room, I didn't know what to do. There was little sense in having a conversation with a person who couldn't respond. Finally, because I loved her so much, I did what I feared and took her hand to pray. I simply said, "Mary, this is Matt. I'm here because I love you. Your grandchildren who love you so much told me you were very sick. We want to do everything we can for you, although there is not much we can do. But Jesus loves you even more than we do, and he can do everything you need. So let my hand become the hand of Jesus, and let him take you wherever he wants to walk with you." Then I prayed quietly for Jesus to take her home to heaven. After a minute of prayer, I left her and visited the other patients.

When I returned by her room, the nurse said, "Why don't you go in and visit Mary?" I answered, "I was already in to see her." The nurse replied, "Yes, but now she is out of her coma and can talk to you."

Mary smiled as I entered and weakly whispered, "You were just in to see me."

"Yes, but how did you know?"

"I've been hearing things but just couldn't talk or move. When you took my hand and asked Jesus to take my hand, he did. We walked together across a beautiful field with flowers and birds. Then at the other side, Jesus said, 'Mary, what can I do for you?' I told him that you made me lonesome for my grandchildren. I wanted to be back with them. So Jesus turned around. He took me back here and I woke up."

I could hardly believe that with my feeble prayer for her happy death, Jesus had brought Mary back to life. I believe that Jesus was able to do so much because I loved Mary so much and my loving hand could enable Mary to trust his hand. My love for Mary overcame my fear of praying *with* another rather than *for* another (1 Jn 4:18). So when I find myself becoming self-conscious and my fear of praying with another returning, I pause until I see how much Jesus and I love that person. Then I usually begin to want to express that love in a simple prayer.

One of my greatest fears in praying with another was that my prayer would raise false expectations and nothing would happen. So now I tell people, "Jesus can do anything—physical, emotional or spiritual healing—but we will only know what he is doing after we pray. He will do whatever most helps us to grow in giving and receiving love because this is always his will. Remain open to anything happening, give thanks for all that is given, and pray to receive more. His healing may be immediate or, as occurs more often, over time as we pray daily."

Why doesn't God always heal totally and immediately? It is a mystery but a mystery due to God's love rather than to his reluctance to heal.[4] When I was with another priest giving a retreat, he shared how a blind woman asked him for prayers since she had inoperable cataracts. This priest and the woman's husband prayed with her and she began to see. So they prayed more but her vision became worse, though it was still better than before the prayer. So my priest friend told the couple that Jesus showed he could heal but it was not his time yet. "Go home and pray five minutes each night for each other. Just ask the other how you should pray and then lay your hand and pray with all the love Jesus places in your heart. Then come back in a month and tell me what has happened."

The couple came back the next month and the woman said, "Now I can see perfectly. But there is an even greater healing that happened because of our nightly prayer together. We were going to get a divorce because we felt we could never love one another again. But our five minutes of loving the other with Jesus showed us how much we really love each other and healed our marriage." Then the priest asked me, "Do you see why Jesus took his time? He wanted not to heal just eyes but this couple's marriage too." Jesus takes his time when we need more love, and in the process of praying for each other, he makes us both great lovers. The blind woman's healing was not just being able to see, but also being freed from hurts and fears so that she could more deeply love God and others. As her husband tried to pray with her as Jesus, he too became a greater lover.

What can we do if we want to love a person as Jesus, but for some reason we cannot pray *with* them? We can begin by praying *for* them, since Jesus' love transcends times and space. I (Sheila) come from a Jewish family, and I have always been hesitant to impose my faith upon my family by suggesting Christian prayer. One of my brothers, Jimmy, has cerebral palsy, is mentally retarded and lives in an institution in a distant state. Jimmy was quite withdrawn as a child, and what I remember most about him was the sadness in his eyes, as if his spirit were trapped within a spastic body and a retarded intellect. Four years ago, I began to pray for Jimmy from a distance. I tried to imagine how alone Jimmy might be feeling. Then I would imagine Jesus standing beside Jimmy, with his arm around Jimmy's shoulders and looking deep inside Jimmy to tell him he was not alone. Finally I'd watch what other ways Jesus wanted to be Jimmy's friend and enter his isolated world.

Last spring I traveled east to visit Jimmy, for the first time since I had begun praying for him. The first thing I noticed about Jimmy was that his eyes were different. They were peaceful and happy. He looked at me as if he somehow knew me, even though he could not remember my name. Then I noticed that everyone was stopping to talk to Jimmy, and that he responded to all this love with smiles and hugs. Jimmy's social worker told me that during the past four years (the years during which I had prayed) he had gradually come out of himself to such an extent that now he is the most popular patient at the school because he gives and receives so much love. She also said that his muscular coordination and his mental ability have improved. A recent letter from her adds, "His vocabulary is growing by leaps and bounds and he appears happy." Although Jimmy still has a partially spastic body and retarded intellect, I believe that his lonely, isolated heart was healed through prayer so that he could become a lover.

For healing prayer what is needed is not an expert but a lover. Jesus uses non-expert lovers such as Sr. Gloriana's mentally ill patients, Joan's parents or a blind spouse. We can all begin as I did praying for my brother Jimmy or as Matt did praying with Mary, the Sioux grandmother. "All" even includes you. Perhaps you can ask Jesus to show you one friend you really love with whom he is calling you to pray. Then spend a few minutes thanking Jesus for all the ways you are grateful for your friend. As you continue through this book, you might wish to pray *for* your friend as I did for my brother Jimmy. All this will increase your love until you really want to ask if your friend wishes you to pray *with* him or her. Then let Jesus within you love your friend through silent touch or with words. Both you and your friend will never be the same.

---

4. In his excellent book *Healing* (Notre Dame: Ave Maria, 1974), Francis MacNutt has a chapter, "Eleven Reasons Why People Are Not Healed."

Chapter 1
The Healing Power of Scripture Prayer

Have you ever prayed alone or with another and found that God didn't seem to be doing or saying anything? In praying the Scriptures where we have the actions and words of Jesus, we don't have to continue guessing what Jesus wants to do and say.

This last year I (Dennis) didn't know what to do or say when a destitute woman came so filled with shame that she covered her face with her shawl. Finally she said, "I want to tell you something that I've never told anybody else before." After she told me her secret sin which she thought nobody would ever forgive, she cried and cried as if she had no hope. So I asked Jesus when in his life he had met such a problem and what he had done. Feeling her shame and hearing her tears, it struck me that she was weeping at my feet like the woman in the house of Simon the Pharisee (Lk 7:36–50).

So I placed my hand on her hair and I whispered in her ear, "God wants to share with you a secret. One time a woman cried so much that she washed Jesus' feet with her tears, and then she dried them with her hair. Jesus said to that woman, 'You love much because you have been forgiven much.' Your secret is that you are that woman and you can love much now because you have been forgiven much." With that, she looked into my eyes, and she cried again. But this time the tears were tears of gratitude from being loved so much. She had heard the secret. Two days later she gave me a silver dollar and said, "My husband on his deathbed gave me two silver dollars. I want to give you this silver dollar because through you Jesus loved me as deeply as my husband loved me when he gave them to me." She now knows from her experience and from the Scriptures that whenever Jesus meets shame and tears, he always responds as he did at the house of Simon the Pharisee and she is welcome there too.

This method of listening to Jesus respond from the Scriptures is nothing new, but the way Jesus chose to heal the discouraged disciples at Emmaus (Lk 24:13–35). Jesus simply used the Scriptures to trade hearts. He let them tell him all that burdened their hearts such as how the one they hoped would free Israel had met instead an ignominious death and dashed all their hopes. Then when they had told Jesus all they were feeling, Jesus told them what he felt and how the Scriptures said this was necessary for the Messiah to enter new glory. They found that their own hearts began burning with the hope in Jesus' heart as he explained the Scriptures (Lk 24:32). Then they returned to their community and used the Scriptures just as Jesus did to bring new hope to the discouraged. The Scriptures are not just for the original situation two thousand years ago but, when used as Jesus did, bring life to wherever there is the same situation or struggle. Jesus has the same attitudes and reactions today as he did two thousand years ago and he wants to trade hearts with every person who has a heavy heart.

We trade hearts all the time with others. Sometimes, for instance, when I go to a prayer meeting, I think, "I am really tired and would rather be home in bed early. I can't stand this emotional singing." But then I try to join in the songs of others that praise God more than I want to praise. I begin to catch their praise until, by about the fourth song, I am no longer forcing myself but the praise rises from my heart too. Or again, if I am tired, I can be with a negative, depressed person and walk away also feeling negative and depressed. That is the process of trading hearts. In Scripture prayer we trade hearts with Jesus until we are thinking and feeling as he does in that passage.

Families do this too. Last night a wife shared how hard it is for her to emotionally be up when her husband is down with financial struggles. But if she can keep hope, he catches it too. We trade hearts with those we love. But what if both are looking to the other for life and unable to give it? Then look together to Jesus. Two friends, a doctor and his wife, get up daily at 5:00 A.M. to listen to Jesus speak his Scriptures to them. They begin by reading the day's Gospel aloud, or sometimes they take another passage that Jesus puts in their hearts. Then they take the next twenty minutes in silence to absorb the heart of Jesus in that passage, following which they share with each other in just a few words what moved them in that passage. Finally, after listening and responding to each other, they pray with each other in whatever way the other asks for prayer. This hour of quality time spent sharing hearts with Jesus and each other has so changed their relationship that they choose to spend an hour of quality time with each of their twelve children every week. During that hour they will do whatever the child wants to do and especially whatever will help that child share his or her heart. To have this family time, this doctor chose to reduce his medical practice by about a fourth. Their family has less income but so much more life.

Deep hurts are healed through Scripture prayer not only when prayed with another but also when prayed alone. A few years ago I noticed that a priest friend, who had struggled all his life with depression, was now changed and free. So I asked him what made the difference. He shared how he had recently made a retreat.

> For two yours I told my director how I didn't like myself—how I was born in an alcoholic family, how my father abandoned me, how I failed to finish my dissertation, and finally how I failed to get tenure. Everything I tried, I failed at. And look at me. I'm eighty pounds overweight. I'm the ugliest man I know. But my director just looked at me and said, "Spend the next day watching how Jesus responds to the ugliest person in Scripture, the Gerasene demoniac." I did that the next day and for the rest of my eight-day retreat. I could hardly believe how much Jesus loved that wild man. He brought out the beauty hidden in him until he could even be sent out to preach to others. Then I began to see how Jesus was using even my background of alcoholism and being an orphan to help me work with the Indian people who were plagued by alcoholism and frequently lost family members. I could have real compassion for them because I had grown up in a family like theirs and I could make them my family. The turning point was when I saw how Jesus treated a person who was just like me. Then I could start to love myself too, and start to love the others who were around me. For the first time I am really happy and glad to be me.

Such changes made through Scripture prayer are so deep that they can last a lifetime and change the world. When we were in England during the Brixton riots, the British televised the story of Daddy King, the father of Martin Luther King. Daddy King shared how his own conversion occurred. As a child, Daddy King had to eat at the back door while his white plantation playmates were fed at the table. At age three this struck home and he hated white people with a growing vengeance.

One day when he was about eighteen, he looked at a cross in his church. Deep in his heart he heard the words of Jesus from the cross, "Father, forgive them. They know not what they are doing" (Lk 23:34). At that moment Daddy King was overwhelmed with a desire to forgive white people no matter what they had done to him and to his black people. Those words melted away his mountain of prejudice and planted the seeds of non-violent resistance that loves an enemy. His son, Martin Luther King, inherited this deep forgiveness and led blacks to love their enemy even when attacked by police brutality. That living out of the Scriptures healed American hearts too, and soon the Civil Rights Act became a reality.

Since Scripture prayer has such power, I (Matt) visited the Holy Land to further immerse myself in praying over the Gospel stories. I tried to walk in the footsteps of Jesus and absorb his mind and heart. I was moved most not while at the great shrines but at the second station of the cross. At this station I bought some rosaries. When I paid for the rosaries, the shopkeeper substituted a sealed plastic bag containing broken, cheap rosaries I would never buy. He obviously was hoping that I wouldn't open the bag until I was back in the United States, but I opened it outside his store. So I returned to demand either the rosaries he said he was selling me or that he return my money. He grinned and said, "A sale is a sale. Sorry." So I kept chasing his customers away by sharing with them my grievance until he finally returned my money. All was rectified.

But I couldn't forgive him and I continued to delight in warning his customers not to buy from him. I felt so good catching his dishonesty. I wanted to rub his nose in the dirt so he would not take advantage of more tourists. I hated his wrongdoing and I disliked him rather than hating the sin and loving the sinner by forgiving him. Finally in desperation, I asked Jesus to help me forgive what I couldn't forgive. Then it struck me that the store was at the second station where Jesus forgave all who struck and took advantage of him as he took his cross. Rather than fight back, he chose to hold the forgiving cross. So I stood with Jesus at the second station until I could choose to forgive that merchant and had Jesus' heart within. When I could see how Jesus forgave the men who put the cross on his shoulders, I had to laugh at my struggle to forgive the man who made me carry broken rosaries. The change was so sudden that it showed me how much I need to get into Jesus' mind rather than just into my own will power.

That experience also showed me how the events in Jesus' life become alive when I bring my current struggle to Jesus and ask him where he or another in the Gospels felt the same as I do. Only when I knew how difficult it was to be taken advantage of could I understand the second station and know Jesus' heart. So now before I begin my daily prayer, I often ask Jesus to show me what I am feeling and when he or another felt the same. Then the Scripture passage he leads me to becomes alive and healing.

Every two weeks our Jesuit community gathers and shares how we are struggling or growing and where we are with Jesus in the midst of that struggle or growth. So I often ask Jesus what I have felt the past two weeks and then I ask him when he felt the same so that I can discover what mystery in his life I am living out. A month ago I returned home after eight months on the road and was so grateful to be home rather than on a plane. (That week a Korean airliner flying from Anchorage to Seoul was shot down on the same route I had been flying four weeks earlier.) I felt like Jesus wanting to sit all night with Mary at Bethany. That mystery showed me what Jesus would choose and helped me to resist my temptation to answer eight months of mail with my hard working ''Martha'' side and miss the joy of being ''Mary'' sitting with my Jesuit brothers.

But two weeks later, I discovered that I had to leave home a month ahead of schedule to write this book in St. Louis. I find the discipline of writing difficult and would rather do anything else. Now I was in the mystery of Jesus telling the others that they must all go up to Jerusalem to suffer (Mk 8:31–38). Jesus clearly was choosing St. Louis, but I was like Peter resisting the cross. I stood with Jesus until like Jesus I could also choose the cross rather than wish I were going elsewhere. Even hot St. Louis is hardly as bad as Jerusalem. I also saw how Jesus walked to Jerusalem not out of a desire to suffer but because of the people he loved such as the disciples he wanted to accompany him. So each day I begin this writing by picturing the people I love since it is for them I want to write this book. This is only Chapter 1, but so far I am filled with their love and eager to write—even now at midnight.

Maybe then it is time to stop and ask what you are feeling now and when Jesus or another in the Gospel felt the same way. Maybe you are like the silver dollar woman ashamed and weeping at Jesus' feet. Maybe like Daddy King hearing the words from the cross or like myself at the second station, you are struggling to forgive a stinging hurt. Or hopefully you are grateful and eager to celebrate life at Bethany or the transfiguration. Perhaps the following prayer will help you to find the Scripture mystery you are living now so that you can trade hearts with Jesus and be powerfully healed. Perhaps you are to be another Daddy King.

EMMAUS PRAYER

1. Close your eyes and imagine yourself walking down the road to Emmaus. Feel the stones under your feet and smell the stifling dust as the perspiration drips down your forehead from the beating sun.

2. Share with Jesus your strongest feelings or whatever is most on your mind. If you don't know what to share, perhaps feel the tension in your body and see what it is saying.

3. When you are finished, look into the eyes of Jesus and take in what he is saying to you from the Scriptures where he or another felt the same way. Breathe in his response until your heart is burning with all that is in his heart.

Chapter 2
Healing Prayer and the Stages of Friendship
(Prayer with Judy)

Did you ever wonder what you could do to pray better? Or did you ever wonder after a prayer whether or not you had prayed well?

I (Dennis) used to have many different criteria for whether or not I had prayed well. When I was tired, I thought I had prayed well if I had avoided distractions and felt more centered and relaxed. Good prayer was when I had a backache, and after giving over to Jesus the situations I was carrying, I no longer experienced the back pain; or good prayer was when I discovered why I was reacting so strongly to a person who wrote me a long letter each week. At other times I thought I had prayed well if I got an insight into the homily I needed to prepare or into the counseling session I was going to have with a couple considering divorce. Though it is helpful to get things done in prayer, there is a deeper criterion for praying well.

Working out on the Indian missions gave me a different criterion for whether or not I had prayed well. I found that most of the Sioux Indian students who were struggling with alcohol and drugs didn't change much even though we gave them methods to get themselves centered and relaxed, insights into why they were the way they were, or suggestions on how to relate better to others such as their parents. Though some of these things helped, the most lasting changes seemed to happen to them when they fell in love. When a girl looked into a boy's eyes and said, ''I love you,'' so often the shocked boy began to change. Not only did he start to comb his hair, but frequently he would stop drinking or stop taking drugs and look for a job so that he could think about supporting someone he loved.

Perhaps what empowered the Indian students to change is the same thing that my novice master tried to tell me fifteen years earlier. When I asked ''What can I do in order to pray better?'' he responded, ''Prayer is not doing something but being with Someone.'' The

measure for good prayer is the same as that for good friendship (or married love), the depth of loving commitment to Someone. If through my prayer, I grow in loving this Someone (Father, Jesus, Mary, etc.), then I have prayed well and can expect that prayer to transform me as much as love relationships transformed my Sioux students. How can Scripture prayer with another lead to this kind of deep friendship? How can it be a prayer that is not doing something but being with Someone? This chapter will attempt an answer by a focus first on how praying with another leads to deeper friendship with Someone, and second, on what stages of friendship we move through in prayer when loving this Someone.

Praying with Another

Frequently people have told me that when they pray alone not much seems to happen. Yet when they pray with another much happens. What are the dynamics in praying with another that frequently make prayer more alive?

On our last visit to the Indian reservation, a friend Ann helped me understand these dynamics. Ann had been an alcoholic for many years. She had prayed for herself frequently, asking Jesus to take this problem from her. When we asked her what finally helped, Ann recalled one evening when she was shaking with the DT's. Two people found her and loved her even as she was shaking. When they offered to pray with her, Ann knew that God loved her at least as much as these two people did, and she was able to pray with them and ask a loving God for help. Ann described three things that made her prayer with them different from the praying she had done on her own.

First, as she felt Jesus' love flowing through their hands and into her, Jesus' love at last became bigger than her problem. From that moment on Ann knew that Jesus, like her two friends, would stand by her and do anything for her.

Second, as she prayed aloud, she found that as she heard her own prayer, she could tell immediately which of the thoughts and feelings were only shallow wishes and which were deep convictions. As she heard herself say, "I want you Jesus more than I want booze," she was surprised at the conviction in her voice and knew she had expressed the deepest yearning in her heart. She could finally admit that the reasons she had given herself for drinking were indeed rationalizations and had no place in her heart.

Third, as those praying with her prayed with Jesus' mind and heart and then began to give thanks, cry, or even laugh, she found that she could experience Jesus as one who gave thanks, cried, or laughed with her. She found that her tears (i.e., at being abandoned by others) were not just her tears but the way Jesus was crying. As those praying with her began to respond, she experienced concretely how Jesus might respond. No longer was Jesus someone who was sending her these trials, but Someone going through them with her. In praying with her two friends, Jesus had for the first time become a lover and a friend. That love was strong enough to get Ann to quit drinking and to join Alcoholics Anonymous. Ann now has a prayer group primarily for those in Al-Anon or Alcoholics Anonymous and is teaching them to pray with each other that they might also experience the loving and healing God that she met. But friendship with God in prayer can deepen more readily not only when we pray with another but also when we allow the prayer to move through various stages of friendship.

Stages of Friendship in Prayer

When we pray with another, the stages in the process of prayer which lead to deeper friendship with God are the same as those in the development of any friendship:

(1) Polite conversation.
(2) Sharing the other's world.
(3) Sharing our own world.
(4) Becoming the other.

Through Scripture prayer, the prayer of trading hearts with Jesus or another person in Scripture, we can experience these stages of friendship. For example, last year Dennis prayed with Judy for the healing of her grief. Judy's mother died of cancer three years ago. Judy told us that what pained her even more than the loss of her mother was the horror of the painful death itself. Judy kept reliving the trauma of seeing her mother hooked up to a respirator, struggling for breath and experiencing terrible thirst. After her mother's death, Judy was left with grief and fear—fear of hospitals, death, illness, etc. The unanswered question in Judy's heart was, "How could a loving God allow such a painful death?" To answer that, God took her through the four stages of friendship in prayer.

Polite Conversation

When I (Sheila) meet a stranger, I talk at first about the world outside us such as mutual friends, the weather, the news, etc. With a friend or with God I may move back to this level of relationship when a hurt comes between us that I don't want to talk about. I have a choice between letting the hurt cause us to regress to the level of polite conversation or move us to a deeper level of intimacy. Blocks in friendship are the key to deeper friendship if we begin to talk about what separates us and allow our alienation to be turned into understanding and compassion.

When Judy came to Dennis for prayer, she could talk to God about her children, her husband's job, the weather, her prayer group, etc. But Judy's friendship with God was blocked because she could not share with him the question that really mattered to her, "How could a loving God allow such a painful death?"

Sharing the Other's World

Blocks in friendship begin to dissolve and growth comes when we realize we have something in common with the other. We can admire and respect another person, but we cannot be friends with someone who seems "above" us. Discovering the other's humanness draws us to him or her far more than impressive accomplishments. We need to know that another person has been through some of the same things we have and thus can understand how we feel. God, who wanted us for his friends, "became like us in all things but sin" (Heb 4:15). The Gospels tell us about all the things Jesus went through so we can find an opening for friendship, a place where we have something in common with him and so can trust him to know how we feel.

In the prayer with Judy, Dennis began by inviting her to get in touch with her feelings about her mother's death. Dennis' attitude of loving attentiveness helped Judy to know that God too cared about how she felt. Thus Judy felt safe enough to share the hurt that was keeping her at the level of polite conversation with God: How could a loving God allow such a painful death?

After Judy had talked briefly about her feelings of fear and helplessness as she watched her mother's painful death, Dennis encouraged Judy to share Jesus' world by going to a time when Jesus or another in Scripture felt the same way. Judy joined Mary at the foot of the cross, watching as Jesus died a painful death, struggling for breath and experiencing terrible thirst. Since Judy had experienced the same painful death with her mother, she could enter the scene with all her senses, even repeating Jesus' words which were so like her own mother's words: "I thirst."

While Judy stood with Mary and talked to her about Jesus' death, she began to feel how Mary felt. Judy felt very close to Mary, knowing that Mary suffered at the death of her Son just as Judy suffered at the death of her mother. Judy let Mary cry against her, as she realized for the first time that Mary too was sometimes in need of comfort.

Sharing Our Own World

As we discover what we have in common with another, our trust begins to grow and, perhaps hesitantly, we begin to share more deeply our own world. If our thoughts and feelings are received with reverence and care, we can risk going further and share our deepest fears, fragile dreams, mistakes, hurts, and even our guilt that says, "I'm sorry; forgive me."

Before our prayer with her, Judy had always thought of Mary as distant and "perfect," unable to understand the realities of Judy's world, and therefore as someone with whom Judy couldn't really share herself. For Judy, the words of the rosary were a form of polite conversation. After joining Mary at the foot of the cross, Judy saw Mary in her humanness, as one who could understand Judy's world because she had been through some of the same things.

So Dennis encouraged Judy to tell Mary all the things about her mother's death that were hard for her. Judy remembered how frightened she felt in her mother's hospital room. But now as Judy saw that same hospital room, Mary was there holding her, and so Judy could recall the scene without fear. Dennis asked Judy to remain in the hospital room with Mary for a few moments and to continue breathing in Mary's love.

After remaining in that room and filling herself with Mary's love, Judy asked Mary to be with her at the moment when her mother died. Judy saw Mary bring Jesus into the room also. Judy told her mother that she loved her and wished she didn't have to suffer. Judy then saw Jesus holding his arms out to her mother, and her mother looking happy and full of light, as if she were forgetting about the pain already. Judy saw her mother smile, an assuring smile that said, "I'm really O.K." Then her mother walked out the door of the hospital room with Jesus. She looked back as if to say, "Don't worry."

As friendship grows, friends find many ways of saying "don't worry"—a box of their favorite freshly baked cookies, a long distance call at just the right moment, or an offer to babysit small children when our friend needs a day to herself. So often in healing prayer, Jesus, Mary or another will reach out with the special care and creativity of a friend, in ways that surprise us. As Judy rested in Mary's arms in the hospital room, Mary surprised Judy by reaching out to touch the baby Judy was carrying in her womb. This touch filled the longing in Judy's heart for a mother to help care for her child. Judy could then close the prayer by asking that her new feeling of closeness to Mary might continue and that Mary might continue to be her new mother.

Judy told us that her mother's painful death no longer seemed like a "weird punishment" sent by God. Now Judy knew that Jesus and Mary were going through that death with her and were "just as concerned as I was," because they had been through the same thing at the foot of the cross. As Judy looked at her mother's death through Jesus' and Mary's eyes, she was moving toward the fourth stage of friendship, becoming the other.

Becoming the Other

The deepest prayer and friendships move even beyond just being together with someone to becoming that person. After fifty years of a close marriage, my grandfather died leaving my grandmother alone with only memories and tears. But my grandfather lived on in her because their years together had made them think, feel and even speak as one. She knew his mind and heart intimately and knew exactly to whom he would give his watch or what he wanted to say to each of his grandchildren and friends. When she spoke it was as if my grandfather were speaking and he was still with us when she said, with his businesslike voice,

"Wipe your feet." Although my grandmother could only become like my grandfather, in prayer we not only can become like Jesus but can even be Jesus.

Although I (Dennis) agree with my novice master that prayer is being with Someone, deep prayer goes beyond being with Jesus to even being Jesus. As I pray over the Gospels, rest with Jesus, or receive him in the Eucharist, I gradually become him with his mind, heart, and reactions. So whether I am saying the Lord's Prayer or bouncing a child on my knee, I find myself saying the phrases or stroking the child not as I did before but as Jesus within me now wants to do. Prayer becomes not only talking to Jesus outside myself, but letting Jesus within me more and more talk to the Father. Prayer immerses me in the mind and heart of Jesus until I discover that he is my deepest identity. As St. Paul said, "It is no longer I who live but Christ lives within me" (Gal 2:20). Prayer is letting the same spirit of Jesus that is within me cry out, "Abba" (Rom 8:15), and knowing that the Father is looking at me and crying out, "Jesus." Prayer is not doing something but being with Somone until I become him—until I become Jesus.

Perhaps, especially for women, it is easier to think of becoming Mary filled with the Spirit rather than becoming Jesus. Just as Judy in the hospital room was able to take on Mary's thoughts and feelings until she had Mary's view of her mother's death, Judy later found when she returned home to her family that she continued to think and feel like Mary. Judy became aware that Mary was less and less a person outside of her and more someone who was dwelling (united to the indwelling Jesus) within her. For example, at home Judy has a picture of Mary weeping, with the words "And a sword shall pierce your heart" (Lk 2:35) written across the bottom. Whenever a crisis happens, Judy looks at the picture and then she feels the heart of Mary within her pierced by a sword. Finally, Judy draws on the strength coming from Mary's heart, until she is able to respond to the crisis as Mary within her wants to respond. For instance, before Dennis' prayer with Judy, she was always frightened by illness. Even a phone conversation in which a friend would speak about someone's illness would fill Judy with fear. Judy had lived with the continual fear that her own children would get sick. Now when one of Judy's children is ill, as Judy glances at Mary's picture, she can respond to her child by holding and caring for it as Mary within her desires. But even a greater healing for Judy is knowing that even if her fear of sickness would return, she could still be Mary. Having experienced Mary's weariness and fears under the cross, Judy no longer feels she has to be the perfect strong mother, but rather is comfortable sometimes being the weary and fearful Mary who, standing under the cross, gathers strength from her Son. To the extent that Judy becomes Mary, she grows closer to Jesus who is always at the center of Mary's heart.

In our prayer with Judy, the hurt of her mother's death was healed. But, more importantly, Judy has entered into a friendship with Jesus and Mary that will sustain her for the rest of her life. The criterion for prayer is not just getting things done by healing hurts, but how much we enter into a deeper level of friendship until we finally become the Other.

PRAYER FOR EXPERIENCING JESUS AS FRIEND

1. Read Luke 10:39: "Martha had a sister named Mary who seated herself at Jesus' feet and listened to his words."

2. Let Jesus show you a friend who loves you much. (Perhaps you may wish to sit with that friend in front of a fireplace. Hear the logs crackle.)

3. Take deep breaths and fill yourself with the love of that friend.

4. Let Jesus join you and draw in his love as Mary did while seated at Jesus' feet.

Chapter 3
Blocks to Healing Prayer

When we can't pray, what is the most likely reason? There may be many reasons. We may need to simplify our prayer by thinking less, or speaking less, or by returning to a time where we can rest in Jesus' love. At other times we may need to change sinful patterns or compromises. We may need to take time to live a balanced life or take more care in providing the proper atmosphere for prayer (see Appendix B, "Scripture Prayer Helps"). But many times we do all these helpful things, and our prayer is still as laborious and tasteless as chewing concrete. Then the most common block in prayer is often our failure to get in touch with feelings, especially "negative" feelings. It is easy to ignore feelings such as discouragement over not being able to pray or the everyday feelings of fear, anger, and guilt. We may keep wishing these feelings would all go away rather than letting Jesus love us with our negative feelings.

In deciding not to ignore negative feelings but rather to heal the hurtful situations which trigger them, we may find ourselves moving through the same five stages (denial, anger, bargaining, depression, and acceptance) that a person moves through in facing the greatest hurt, death.[1] Such was the case of Linda who found her prayer blocked at each of those five stages until she could face yet another layer of negative feelings involved in trying to forgive a relative who sexually abused her beginning at age ten. Linda came to us after fourteen years of therapy for suicidal depression. She had the mannerisms and gestures of a child, looking frightened and withdrawn as she sat curled up in the corner of a chair. She wore her hair short and straight, in a childish way. She always dressed in slacks, like a tomboy. It was as if her psychosexual development had stopped at the age of ten. What follows is an account of Linda with a special focus on what helped and what blocked her prayer as she moved through those five stages in healing the hurt with her relative. (Since a person can be in many of the five stages at one time, what follows is a simplified account of Linda's experience, in which we have taken some liberty with the exact chronology of events.)

First Stage: Denial

Those in the first stage, denial, either deny that they were hurt or, like Linda, deny that they can do anything about it. As Linda sat curled up in the chair, she could repeat the same list of hurts that she had told others for fourteen years. It was as if her curled up posture and the fourteen years of therapy were telling everyone, "I am powerless. I have been hurt and will have to carry those wounds forever." In this stage Linda's prayer was blocked because she was angry at God for having abandoned her as a youngster and she doubted that God cared about her.

With Linda we did not start by praying with her nor did we encourage her to focus on her hurt. What people in the denial stage usually need is to be filled with love, to be built up on the inside so that eventually they will have the inner resources to face the hurtful situation. With most people in the denial stage, it is not that they haven't received love, but rather that they haven't taken it in. So we asked Linda to keep a journal and each day to write her answer to the question: When during the day did you receive love or grow in love? When Linda looked puzzled at the question, I (Dennis) asked her if she had received love during the half-hour she was with me. So that half-hour became the first entry in her book as I invited her to write down

---

1. These stages are based on Elisabeth Kübler-Ross, *On Death and Dying* (New York: Macmillan, 1969). For how to move through the stages in forgiving another cf. Dennis and Matthew Linn, *Healing Life's Hurts* (New York: Paulist, 1978).

when during that session she felt most loved and then to take a few deep breaths and receive it.

Linda continue to write in her journal each day, telling Jesus about the moments when she had felt loved. As she listened for the Lord's response, he kept speaking to her about love. Love became more and more the focus of Linda's attention. In her journal Linda also told Jesus that she did not want to share her feelings with him about how she had been hurt. He told her it was all right for her not to share her feelings and continued to speak to her about love. Because Linda felt accepted by Jesus in her unwillingness to share her feelings, she was able to move on to the next stage.

Second Stage: Anger

In the stage of anger, a person like Linda begins to blame others for hurting or destroying her. Linda's first target was God. She was angry at God for abandoning her when she was sexually abused at the age of ten. She wrote in her journal how she felt about God:

> Linda: I hate your guts. Get out of my life. I don't want you. You weren't there when I needed you. And I suppose you are going to leave me again because I am cussing you out.
> Jesus: Go ahead and cuss me out.
> Linda: Go to hell, you and the whole world.
> Jesus: I see how deeply you were hurt. That army of anger is strong and has many soldiers. Fire on me with your many guns. I can take it all. I want to take this army of rage and anger and transform it into an army of love.

After many experiences like this of expressing her anger at God, Linda knew that Jesus was willing to take her at her worst, and so she was finally willing, after fourteen years, to face with Jesus the worst moments in her life.

While we were praying with Linda about the worst moments in her life, the experience of sexual abuse beginning at the age of ten, we tried all the different ways we knew to help her to forgive her relative, but Linda remained angry. Her prayer remained blocked until I (Sheila) suggested to her that Jesus too was angry, even outraged, at the ways Linda had been sexually abused. Then, as Linda continued to pray, she saw Jesus become as angry over her body being defiled as he was when his Father's temple was defiled. Linda began to cry, something she was unable to do even during her fourteen years of psychotherapy, tears of relief and gratitude at knowing that Jesus loved her enough to share her anger. As Linda said, "He wants to share all of me with all of my feelings." With her emptiness filled, Linda no longer felt powerless. Knowing that Jesus was present where before there was only emptiness gave Linda the confidence to take the next step in dealing with her hatred of her relative and her hatred of herself.

What heals in prayer at each of the five stages is sharing our negative feelings with Jesus and letting him love us with those feelings, as Linda did. There are four steps in letting the Lord love us with our negative feelings:

1. Feel our feelings, e.g., when Linda let herself be angry at the evil done by the people who abused her.

2. Ask Jesus "When did you feel the same way?" and let him tell us, for example, "I felt this anger in the temple."

3. Let Jesus say and do for us the things he wants to say and do. In Linda's case, Jesus wanted to show his anger on her behalf. In another situation, Jesus might want to be silent and simply hold us. What matters is that we allow Jesus to say and do whatever he wishes for us, as we move through our negative feelings.

4. The fourth step is to watch how Jesus moves through those negative feelings and then do it with him. It was six months before Linda could take this fourth step to join Jesus on Calvary as he was stripped of his garments. There she joined Jesus and watched him forgive the people who abused him until she could forgive, in the same way, her relative.

Frequently in praying with people like Linda, we may move too quickly to the fourth step and try to get people to forgive without first of all allowing them to be loved with their negative feelings. "Negative" feelings are gifts meant to help us resist whatever would harm us or others, and to help us know the depth of forgiveness asked of us as we unite ourselves with Jesus who hates the sin and loves the sinner. Usually when we experience negative feelings, they are the way Jesus within us is hating the sin, as in Linda's case where Jesus within her was angry at the evil of sexual abuse. Healing happens when we feel the negative feelings with Jesus, and then, in the fourth step, watch how he acts with that feeling until we can begin loving the sinner with him.

Third Stage: Bargaining

What blocked Linda's prayer for six months making it impossible for her to forgive her relative? In the third stage of bargaining a person like Linda begins to set up conditions that have to be fulfilled before she will forgive. Linda still wanted "to put him on a guilt trip" so "he'd have to pay" for what he had done. So Linda blocked any prayer for forgiveness until three conditions could be met. Her three bargains were: I will forgive this man *if* he knows how much he hurt me, *if* he will tell me why he did it, and *if* he will apologize to me.

Linda's prayer became unblocked as she worried less about forgiving her relative and instead brought each bargain, with all its negative feelings, to Jesus. For instance, she remembers imagining herself raging, screaming, and beating up her relative as she stood at the foot of Jesus' cross. She asked, "Jesus, how is it that from the cross you can forgive those who have abused you, yet I cannot forgive this man?" Then Linda saw Jesus come down from the cross and put her in his lap. She listened as Jesus began talking with her relative. Jesus told him how much he had hurt Linda. Linda could let go of each bargain (i.e., to have her relative know how much he hurt her) as she saw that her need was understood by Jesus and that Jesus was doing the best he could to see that need filled.

When Linda finally let go of her bargains at the foot of the cross, she said: "I felt a lightness, like a feather, that I had never felt before. The rage, anger, and resentment toward my relative and others left me." She joined Jesus on Calvary where he was stripped of his garments (a form of sexual abuse). Linda watched Jesus as he forgave the people who abused him, and then in the same way she began to forgive her relative who had abused her.

Having forgiven her relative, she allowed his pain to touch her. Rather than seeing her relative as a person who "had to pay" for what he had done, she saw him as he now was, alone and dying of lung cancer. A short time later Linda helped gather this man's relatives and encouraged them to forgive him. Linda felt that if they could do this, the dying man (who for the last three months because of vocal chord tumors and a respirator machine had been unable to speak) would be able to speak again. The man's relatives all forgave him. To their amazement, the next day he was taken off the respirator, coughed up a phlegm-like substance, and was again able to speak. He spent some time with each member of the family, being reconciled and telling them how he loved them. Several days later he died peacefully. In the stage of bargaining, as we share our bargains and the negative feelings behind them, our prayer of forgiveness becomes unblocked and we can experience the healing power of forgiveness as Linda's relatives did.

Fourth Stage: Depression

After Linda helped lead those relatives in forgiving the dying man, she began asking herself, "Why didn't I ever do this before?" In the fourth stage, that of depression, a person like Linda blames herself for ways she contributed to the hurt and for ways she let the hurt affect her life. Whereas in the anger stage Linda saw the hurt as all the man's fault, in the depression stage she saw the hurt as all her own fault.

The five stages may overlap, and even during our first prayer, as Linda was struggling through the anger stage to forgive her relative, she was also struggling through the depression stage to forgive herself. So we asked Linda to enter the scene of Jesus forgiving the adulterous woman (Jn 8:10–11). As Linda entered the scene, she became that adulterous woman. But she also saw herself as a member of the crowd, wanting to throw the biggest stone of all at the adulterous woman and refusing to put it down no matter what Jesus said or did. Although we wanted Linda to forgive herself and put the stone down, we finally realized that Jesus wanted to love her with that stone and was telling her that she didn't have to put it down until she was ready. Linda told us later that the stone represented her sexual identity, which she hated, and that the most important thing Jesus did for her was allow her to keep the stone until she was ready to put it down. Linda was eventually able to move through the depression stage because Jesus showed her it was all right to be there and all right to hold her stone of self-hatred until she was ready to put it down.

Each time Linda prayed, she was blocked in putting down the stone because she couldn't love her sexual identity and could not believe that Jesus could love her in that area of her life either. Sometimes when people are blocked in prayer because they are unable to receive Jesus' love in an area of their life, what helps is to share that area of life with a friend whose acceptance of them shows how Jesus accepts them. During the next week, Linda came to see me (Sheila) and a friend of mine, Sr. Marie. Linda told us about her stone: how she hated herself, how she wished to punish herself, and how she was afraid to get in touch with her grief over all the things she had done wrong. Linda told us that she hated herself because she believed it was her fault that her relative had abused her, and because of her own subsequent sexual acting out with men. Then she told us the deepest reason for her self-hatred, something which (outside of a quick, rote confession)[2] she had never shared before: as a teenager, she had abused small children in the same ways she herself was abused.

Linda had finally shared with us the thing she hated most in herself, the thing she believed could never be forgiven. This was the reason that her prayer was blocked and that she could not put down the stone. Linda hated herself as a woman, and she could not imagine that Sr. Marie or I, as women, could ever accept her. But Sr. Marie and I both felt a deeper love for her than ever before. For the next weeks, Linda would call us every day and ask the same questions: "Do you hate me? How could you possibly love me after the awful things I've done?" Each day we would respond by telling Linda once more of our love for her. Gradually Linda began to believe that if Sr. Marie and I could love her when we knew the worst things about her, then maybe she could put down her stone and let Jesus love her too.

Now that Linda had risked sharing with us her deepest negative feelings, the thing she hated most about herself, it became important to assure her (even through daily phone calls) that she was part of us and we would not abandon her. Not only did she want to feel part of Sr. Marie and me, but, as we continued to meet with Linda for prayer, she wanted to feel part of Jesus' family too. Thus each week we asked Jesus to take her home to be loved by his parents, Mary and Joseph. She felt welcomed in their home with her stone, just as we had welcomed her. In our prayer, we asked that Mary and Joseph become Linda's adoptive parents. We also asked that their wholesome love for each other as husband and wife enfold Linda as it did Jesus, penetrating her subconscious mind and memory from the moment of conception, and reforming her sexual identity in light rather than the darkness in which she had been raised.

Although Linda was able to receive some love in this prayer, she still could not put down the stone and also seemed blocked whenever we prayed for light to come into her sexual identity at the moment of conception. Several signs alerted us that Linda might need deliverance prayer to forgive herself and move through the depression stage: (1) her intense reaction to any mention of conception in our prayer (violent crying and a feeling of grief so deep that she feared it would kill her, followed by sudden sleepiness); (2) the compulsive nature of the ways she had abused children, so unlike her own sensitive and caring nature; (3) no breakthroughs in the area of self-hatred, after fourteen years of psychotherapy and months of prayer; (4) her feelings of nausea when she came to the words "deliver us from evil" in the Lord's Prayer.

Most of the time people will move through the five stages and any prayer blocks automatically as they share their negative feelings. But Linda herself recognized the signs we saw and confirmed our suggestion that she might also need deliverance prayer.[3] We waited several more weeks, continuing to fill Linda with the love of the Holy Family so that the light in her would be so great as to allow no further resting place for darkness (Lk 11:24–26).

Fifth Stage: Acceptance

When during the depression stage Linda told Jesus about her stone, she wrote Jesus' response in her journal:

> I want to transform the dark, ugly black stone you hold into a beautiful precious stone, and it will shine and sparkle because of the light of my love that shines down on it.

In the acceptance stage, a person like Linda becomes grateful for the hurt. Jesus not only wants to heal our hurts but he also wants to bring gifts out of them. We move into the acceptance stage the more we see how Jesus has transformed our dark, ugly black stones into beautiful precious stones that can shine and sparkle with light.

After Linda's depression and darkness were gone, she was overwhelmed with gratitude that Jesus could care so much for her. She knew that if Jesus could lovingly bring her through such a deep hurt, then he could love her through anything. Linda now finds herself in the difficult situation of living in a new city, away from old friends and with little money as she searches for work. Yet, Linda feels full of peace, secure that Jesus is with her and would never leave her. This new abiding

---

2. See *Power in Penance* by Michael Scanlan, *op. cit.* Sometimes confession does not seem to heal deeply until the priest receives and lovingly responds as Jesus to what was confessed, especially through healing prayer which touches the hurt behind the sin.

3. For a thorough treatment of deliverance ministry from a psychological, theological and scriptural perspective, see Dennis and Matthew Linn, *Deliverance Prayer* (Ramsey, N.J.: Paulist Press, 1980). See especially pages 22–48, on the need to emphasize deliverance *into* Jesus' love rather than deliverance *from* evil.

sense of peace and security in knowing that Jesus is with her is the gift she is most grateful for in her life.

In the weeks before Linda moved from her previous home, she realized that in her work as a psychotherapist she was reaching a whole new depth with her clients. Linda began to speak freely about her experience of sexual abuse. People who had been hurt in the same way and had never been able to tell anyone received healing as they heard Linda's story and shared their own hurt with Linda so that she could lead them through a similar prayer experience. The more Linda shared what Jesus had done for her, the more grateful she became for how Jesus had made a gift out of her hurt.

Every hurt in life can become a gift just as Linda's did. We have all known alcoholics who have joined Alcoholics Anonymous and have used all they went through in their illness to develop such compassion that they will get up at any hour of the night to help other alcoholics. This year we met a couple who had both been orphans. They wanted to make sure that others didn't have to grow up without parents and thus, during the past forty years, they have become foster parents to over fifteen hundred children. Why do some alcoholics or orphans remain crippled while others become leaders of AA groups or parents to over fifteen hundred children?

Hurts will usually automatically become gifts when we do the same thing Linda did in moving through her hurt. What moved Linda through the five stages of healing her hurt was the same thing that researchers working with psychiatrist Elisabeth Kübler-Ross said would move a person through the five stages of dying: sharing with a significant person who can compassionately hear your feelings.[4] So, too, Linda was able to move through the ways her hurt blocked her prayer at each of the five stages as she shared with a significant other (i.e., Jesus, Sr. Marie, Dennis or myself) what she was feeling.

---

4. Mwalimu Imara, "Dying as the Last Stage of Growth," in Elisabeth Kübler-Ross, *Death: The Final Stage of Growth* (Englewood Cliffs: Prentice-Hall, 1975), p. 160.

The following Sufi tale about a monster watermelon tells us what Linda discovered: monstrous hurts when not compassionately heard bring death; monstrous hurts when heard by a compassionate, significant other bring life.

> Once upon a time there was a man who strayed from his own country into the world known as the Land of the Fools. He soon saw a number of people flying in terror from a field where they had been trying to reap wheat. "There is a monster in that field," they told him. He looked and saw that it was a watermelon. He offered to kill the "monster" for them. When he had cut the melon from its stalk, he took a slice and began to eat it. The people became even more terrified of him than they had been of the watermelon. They drove him away with pitchforks, crying: "He will kill us next, unless we get rid of him." It so happened that at another time another man also strayed into the Land of the Fools, and the same thing started to happen to him. But, instead of offering to help them with the "monster," he agreed with the Fools that it must be dangerous, and by tip-toeing away from it with them he gained their confidence. He spent a long time with them in their houses until he could teach them, little by little, the basic facts which would enable them not only to lose their fear of melons, but even to cultivate them for themselves.[5]

Prayer gets unblocked when we trust that Jesus cares about our watermelons.

PRAYER FOR HEALING NEGATIVE FEELINGS

1. Sit with Peter after he has denied Jesus and remember the moment you too felt furthest from loving Jesus. Feel your shame, fears, etc., as much as Peter feels his.

2. Then let Jesus look at you and Peter. He loves you at your lowest moments with all you feel. Breathe in his love.

3. Jesus doesn't criticize; he simply asks, "Do you love me?" Look into his eyes and slowly give your answer.

---

5. McNeill, Morrison, and Nouwen, *Compassion* (Garden City: Doubleday, 1982), pp. 79–80.

Chapter 4
Healing Through Our Scripture Mystery

As we watch people around the world discover Jesus personally, we see a pattern. After the discovery of Jesus' personal love (perhaps at a retreat, baptism of the Spirit, or crisis in their lives), a honeymoon period often follows for the next year or two. This honeymoon usually focuses on receiving, and sees the community as existing for the purpose of loving us. Then comes the second stage of giving, as we see the needs of others in the community and want to give the love we have received. At this stage we choose to attend a prayer meeting or be with others not because we can receive much but because we can give much. As President Kennedy said, "Ask not what your country can do for you but what you can do for your country." Soon we are on every committee, helping everyone, and become burned out. Our activities become not joys but burdens, tasks we do because no one else is doing them and they need to be done. We find ourselves more irritable, tired, bored, unable to concentrate well, full of worries, less able to dream or pray and always short on time.

These symptoms of burnout may even be projected onto others and onto God. With others, we may feel critical of them, wondering why they can't be as generous and committed as we are. When we pray with people, we may overemphasize using will power and trying harder. With God, we may think he is "testing us" and explain our inner dryness and emptiness as God withdrawing his felt presence to lead us into the "dark night of the soul," when really it is we who have withdrawn from God by becoming too busy doing good and thus unable to be still and receive his love. We may see him as demanding more and more from us, and ready to punish us if we don't "produce."

I once belonged to a prayer group where people became very busy doing good. The leaders began to give teachings and prophecies increasingly focused on God's judgment. They even predicted a coming natural disaster, in the form of an earthquake (which never happened). We were encouraged to work even harder, to prepare for the coming hard times. A wise friend counseled me, "There *is* an earthquake coming . . . an inner earthquake. If those people continue to ignore their own needs and feelings, they will either burn out or blow up." Perhaps the destructive effects of burnout in ourselves and in our relationships with God and others are why St. Ignatius warned that good people are most often tempted by the good—to get overextended in doing good.

When this happens, what helps? Sometimes it helps to see new priorities, to put first our needs and the needs of our family, and to say "no" to other needs. It is time to say "no" to the activities that drain life (like tiring ministry) and "yes" to the activities that bring life (like gardening, hobbies, time with a joyful friend, good music, quiet time to pray and seek priorities). It is a time to once again receive love rather than focus on giving love. We can't give love when we haven't received it.

John too watched burnout in the early Church and wrote the prescription for giving and receiving love, "We love because God has first loved us" (1 Jn 4:19). When we are burdened or burned out, we are to let God love us and just receive in prayer. One way to do this is to return to our favorite Scripture passage and soak up Jesus' strength and healing love. We can give Jesus the burden in our heart and then take in all that is in his heart as did the downcast disciples on the road to

Emmaus. As they heard Jesus' favorite Scriptures proclaiming God's faithful presence in the midst of tragedy, their hearts began to burn within them. Burnout yielded to burning hearts.

For each of us there are special mysteries in Jesus' life that give us life and burning hearts. When Mary was most distraught, she pondered in her heart the memories of Jesus' birth and the memory of finding him in the temple doing the Father's business (Lk 2:19, 51). These mysteries continued to remind her not only how she was specially chosen and entrusted with Jesus but also how the Father would ultimately care for them both even on Calvary. Each of the apostles must also have had special moments they pondered to again experience Jesus' special love: John receiving Mary as mother (Jn 19:26), Peter being forgiven around the lakeshore fire (Jn 21), Thomas being invited to feel Jesus' wounds (Jn 20), and Matthew leaving everything when called (Mt 9:9). Each of the Gospels has special memories pondered by that writer and missed by the others (e.g., only Luke writes about the good Samaritan, the prodigal son, and the ten lepers).

Not only the apostles but also the saints had a special mystery or two that filled them with Jesus' love. What moved St. Ignatius of Loyola at LaStorta was not just the mystery of Jesus carrying his cross, but the idea that the Father would even ask Ignatius to help Jesus carry it. The desire to be with Jesus carrying his cross becomes one of Ignatius' central mysteries. Ignatius invites retreatants in the *Spiritual Exercises* to join Jesus carrying the standard of the cross and to ask for the "third degree of humility" that desires to choose poverty and humiliations with Jesus. Ignatius also tells retreatants to follow his own experience of returning, when in desolation, to whatever Scripture passage or way of meeting Jesus previously gave them consolation. In that passage which especially spoke to them, retreatants can again find Jesus and his direction. The retreatant is also encouraged to taste one passage deeply rather than cover many events in Jesus' life. Ignatius' search for Jesus was inspired by Francis of Assisi who was so overwhelmed by the cross he could not eat a meal if a cross hung in the refectory. Many credit Francis with starting the customs of the stations of the cross and the Christmas crib so that common people could concretely experience more deeply the two main mysteries that spoke to his heart.

Like Francis of Assisi, Teresa of Avila found that concretely picturing a mystery helped her to pray. Teresa complained of a poor imagination and admitted, "I have never succeeded to picture him (Christ) within myself no matter how much I read about his beauty or how many images I have seen of him. I am then like a person who is blind or in darkness."[1] Her favorite aid to focus on Christ was a painting of Jesus and the Samaritan woman that had hung in her childhood home and that she asked to inherit.

> I always carried with me a painting of this episode of the Lord at the well with the words inscribed, "Lord, give me water."[2]

> Oh, how often I remember the living water of which the Lord spoke to the woman of Samaria! I am so fond of that Gospel. I have loved it ever since I was a child—though I did not, of course, understand it properly then, as I do now—and I used often to beseech the Lord to give me that water.[3]

Elsewhere Teresa shares how her life follows the pattern of the Samaritan woman; her previous sins and lukewarmness, her encounter with Christ, her taste of the living water and finally her apostolate of being a woman leading others to Christ. So much life came to Teresa while reflecting on the Samaritan woman passage (Jn 4:4-42) that in her first new foundation, The Convent of St. Joseph, she constructed a well and called it "The Fountain of the Samaritan Woman" and also commissioned an artist to make another Samaritan woman painting. She hoped that making this mystery concretely present in images would give to the other nuns with poor imaginations the life it gave her.

Others like Thérèse of Lisieux (1873-1897) were attracted not so much by the mysteries of Jesus' public life but by the childhood mysteries of Bethlehem and Nazareth. When Thérèse of Lisieux had difficulty praying, she would become like a little child held by Jesus (Lk 18:15-17) and know she was loved not because she could do great deeds but simply because she was a weak child. "Spiritual childhood" became her little way to sanctity by doing little things with love—patiently bearing ill remarks or the fatigue from her tuberculosis, washing a dish with care, or letting Jesus love her when she wanted to pray and could not.

Charles de Foucauld followed in her footsteps from 1897-1900, living Jesus' hidden life as a servant for the Poor Clares in Nazareth. While praying over Je-

1. Teresa of Avila, *Life*, Ch. 9, 6; K. Kavanaugh and O. Rodriguez, *The Collected Works of St. Teresa of Avila* I (Washington, D.C.: ICS, 1976) p. 72
2. *Ibid*, Ch. 30, 19, p. 202.
3. Teresa of Avila, *Life*, ch. 30; E. Allison Peers, *The Complete Works of St. Teresa of Jesus* I (London: Sheed and Ward, 1946), p. 203.

sus' hidden life, Charles wrote what Jesus seemed to say:

> Look at the life I have fashioned for you: could it possibly parallel my hidden life more perfectly? . . . You are living it at Nazareth, unknown, inordinately poor, lonely in your smock and sandals, a poor servant to the poor nuns. Some take you for a laborer of the lowest kind; others think you are an outcast; some think you are perhaps the son of a criminal. Most—nearly all, in fact—take you for a fool. You obey the nuns and the portresses as I obeyed my parents. You give orders to nobody, absolutely no one.[4]

So much did this mystery penetrate his life that he left Nazareth to give fifteen years bringing the hidden Jesus to the Muslim Tuaregs of the North African desert by simply living with them and serving them. Charles felt they would understand Jesus only when they saw him living Jesus' life of service in their midst. Charles also had the gift of opening to others the power of his hidden life mystery, and he founded the Little Brothers and Sisters who as missionaries take even hidden factory jobs to make Jesus present in hidden deeds rather than empty words.

As we receive life from our mystery, our brokenness is healed, and we begin like Charles to touch others with the life from our mystery. A few years ago I met Sr. Ann, a psychiatrist who cares for thirteen schizophrenic children. She shared how she used the Scriptures prayerfully to heal her children.

> When a boy is hallucinating or getting violent, I'll especially sit down with him, put my arm around him and ask him to imagine a warm puppy cuddled in his lap. I have him feel how peaceful the puppy is and tell me what he feels as he holds the puppy. Then I have him imagine that he is holding the puppy in the stable at Bethlehem. I have him tell me what in his imagination he can smell, touch, see and hear. If he hasn't met Mary or Jesus, I might suggest going over and holding their hands or being held by Mary or Joseph. Then I tell him to take deep breaths of all the love that surrounds him and to breathe out any restlessness he might feel. Finally, I ask him to tell me when he is filled with love and has only love to breathe out. Sometimes they just play with Jesus and we don't try any breathing but always they take in healing love and new peace. They are slowly getting better due to the loving community and to this type of prayer.

So I asked Sr. Ann how she discovered this type of Scripture prayer.

> A few years back I realized that I needed prayer for healing because I never wanted to let anybody hug me.

4. J.F. Six, *Spiritual Autobiography of Charles de Foucauld* (Denville: Dimension Books, 1964), p. 48.

I could do it, but my insides would just scream and kind of push people back. And I'd never been able to get at what that was even though I've been through analysis to become a psychiatrist. So I sat down with my friend one day and said, "Let's just ask the Lord to show us what's behind this and how he wants to help us with it." Jesus took both my friend and me back to the same scene. The scene was of myself as a little baby being held by Mary at Bethlehem and just soaking up her love. So I just stayed with that. Then I started thinking, "Well, that's strange. As I look at myself, I'm about six months old. And Jesus was less than a month old at Bethlehem. I should try to make myself smaller." But I couldn't do that. I kept feeling about six months old—that's when I really wanted to sit in Mary's arms and take her love into every part of myself. So I did that for a week in my prayer.

I found as I let Mary hold me as a six-month-old baby, I was being healed and I could let people hug me again. So I went home to my mother and asked her, "Do you remember anything that happened to me when I was about six months old?" She thought a moment and then said, "Yes. When you were about six months old you had a skin rash. It was so painful that I couldn't even bathe you without you screaming. And no one could hold you or touch you." Then I made the connection in my mind that this was what I had been reacting to all those years in which I couldn't be touched. It was letting Mary hold me at six months old and just taking in all the ways I needed to be held at that time that healed me. So now when I pray with others, I often pray in the way I was healed.

When Dennis, Matt and I (Sheila) pray with others, we too return to the place in Jesus' life where we were healed. We became aware of this one day while watching the videotaped prayers upon which this book is based. We noticed how differently each of the three of us prays for healing. Matt's prayers emphasize choosing with Jesus to let hurts become blessings. Dennis' prayers emphasize unconditional forgiveness. And my prayers emphasize nurture and loving care. When we asked one another what Scripture passage meant the most to us, Matt spoke of the Beatitudes, Dennis spoke of the penitent woman who loved much because she was forgiven much, and I spoke of Joseph's and Mary's love for Jesus during his birth and childhood. The place where each of us had received love and healing had become a place from which we could reach out to others. We also saw that as we prayed with others, we asked each person where in Scripture they felt most loved so we would be open to where Jesus might want to love them again rather than imposing our own experience where it didn't fit.

There is no one right way to pray for healing since each of us has been loved differently and we pray out of ways we have been loved and are led by the loving Spirit. We can return to wherever we have been loved in Scripture when we are burned out from the past, overextended in the present or fearful of the future. There we can find Jesus and begin to pray for ourselves or for another when we are uncertain how to pray. When praying with another, Jesus will frequently meet that person in the same mystery that he keeps meeting us. More important than learning techniques to pray with another is meeting Jesus more deeply in the mysteries he most often opens to us. Perhaps we can join Jesus now in whatever mystery in his life has become our favorite for meeting his healing love.

PRAYER TO FIND YOUR HEALING MYSTERY

1. Hold a Bible and thank Jesus for the events of his own life that give you life. (Maybe the Gospel you chose for your wedding day, or would want read at your funeral, or your favorite Scripture passage. If you could be present with Jesus during one event in his life, which would you choose? Where would you feel most loved?)

2. After you have thought of several events, return to the one that makes you feel most loved and be present in it with Jesus, taking in his love.

Chapter 5
Preparation for Healing Prayer: Listening

Although praying with another for healing is important, we often find it difficult to do. What makes it difficult to reach out and to pray for healing? In Luke 8:40-56, the story of Jairus' daughter receiving healing, Jesus and Jairus willingly go to Jairus' home to pray. But the crowd says, "It's useless. Don't go. Why even bother trying?" It's easy for us to have the feelings of the crowd: the fear that something is too big, that if we pray nothing will happen, that this person has been prayed for before so it's senseless to even try again. How can we move through such feelings? In the story of Jairus' daughter, Jesus does a very wise thing. He brings into the girl's room the people who love her the most, her parents. Jesus also brings three of the people who love him the most, Peter, James and John. Healing prayer comes down to loving, and the more love we have the more we can move through any of our obstacles to praying for another.

In praying lovingly for another, we can use the same three steps that Jesus used in praying for Jairus' daughter. The first step (treated in this chapter) is that of listening and discernment. How do we listen so that we know what Jesus might want to do next? Jesus listens to Jairus' request and he hears the voices of the crowd. Then he discerns what he should do. The second step (treated in Chapter 6) is that of praying. How do we pray with another person? Jesus' prayer with Jairus' daughter is a simple address to the child, "Child get up." The third step (to be explored in Chapter 7) is follow-up. How can we encourage another to deepen the healing he or she has received? Jesus begins the process of follow-up when he says to the girl's parents, "Get this child something to eat."

Listening to the Other Person

The first step, that of listening, involves three parts: listening to the other person, listening to ourselves, and listening to Jesus. We'll begin with listening to the other person. Just listening to another is very healing. When we were down in Bogotá, Colombia, we saw in a park a statue of a man who helped the poor during his life. The statue shows the man holding his head with one hand, the elbow resting on his knee, in a listening posture. All day a line of people come up to the statue and whisper in the man's ear all their secrets and problems. Just expressing the problem somehow puts it into a solvable perspective. The people walk away smiling, feeling that their world is a little bit more together because they've been listened to—even by a stone statue.

When we listen to another, we have more to offer than an ear. Psychiatrist Dr. Conrad Baars has said that in praying with another for healing of a painful memory, the most important thing we have to offer is not knowledge of psychology or knowledge of that person's past. The most important thing is how much compassion we have for that person, so that he or she feels loved and affirmed.[1]

Compassion is very different from concern. Concern looks *at* a person as someone separate from us. Concern gives advice and says, "I think you should." It tries to solve a problem. But compassion looks *with* a person and tries to see the world through his or her eyes. While concern sits on a pedestal looking down

---

1. Conrad W. Baars, *Feeling and Healing Your Emotions* (Plainfield: Logos, 1979), pp. 197–98.

on the other, compassion sits reverently at the feet of the other, grateful to be invited into his or her world. Compassion feels the pain of the other and offers not just a head full of good ideas, but a caring heart too. Compassion likes as well as loves the other, and helps that person to believe in himself or herself and his or her goodness as we do. Compassion is healing because it is based on an unconditional love that says, "Even if you don't change, I'm going to be with you as Jesus because I love you and because I feel what you are going through."

When I listen compassionately, people will feel the warmth of my love and usually be able to open up and share their problem just as a flower opens in warm sunlight. But sometimes a person may come and say, "I'm depressed," and yet not know what causes it. With such a person I can ask, "When did it begin? When is the last time you remember not feeling depressed? What seems to contribute to it?" I can also find out the other side, of what has helped in the past, by asking questions like, "What helps? What do you do differently on the better days? How has it helped you to pray before when you felt this way?" Knowing what has helped a person in the past can tell me what may help in the future. This is not the time for giving advice or saying how someone else was helped. My comments should help the other clarify and uncover further his or her experience, and not try to solve it before it is heard and understood.

If I really like another and listen compassionately, the person may even share what he or she has never been able to share previously. When another entrusts me with confidential areas, I am bound to keep this sharing totally confidential just as would a doctor, lawyer or priest hearing confessions. If I feel the need to consult another person with greater experience in ministry, then I should ask permission of the one I have listened to. A person who finds that what was shared privately has become public knowledge will have difficulty ever again trusting another into his or her inner world.

Listening with compassion heals powerfully. The book *Son Rise* by Barry Kaufman describes how his son Raul was called out of his autistic world by compassionate listening and love.[2] At seventeen months, autistic Raul still had not discovered a world outside himself. He had never spoken, responded with a gesture, or even made eye contact with another person. He wanted to be left to his routines of rocking, staring

into space, and spinning objects. But his mother decided she would enter his world even if Raul could not enter hers. For seventy-five hours each week she tried to imitate him spinning plates or staring for an hour into space until she began to feel his imprisonment in autism. As she put aside all the ways she wanted him to be different and tried to love him where he was, she discovered his language of sounds expressing contentment, dislike and needs. One day after spinning plates for eleven hours with Raul, she caught his first fleeting side glance at her that said, "Thank you for being with me."

Once she knew his world and could even guess his next move, Raul's mother began to share even more her beautiful world of love that he had noticed for a split second. She spent hours lovingly stroking Raul in his own language of touch. When he wanted the stimulus of music, she put the cassette tape player behind her so he would have to stare at her while staring at the music. She fed him at eye level so that in looking at a cookie he finally looked into her eyes. He was finally coming out of his world into another. Now he wanted touch, and he wanted his mother when the music was behind her. Raul began to learn, and at an incredible pace. At twenty months he had still tested out at an eight-month level in language, social skills, etc. But by twenty-four months he had caught up to normal development on half the tests and on the other half he tested at thirty to thirty-six months. By the age of two and a half Raul was speaking sentences of fourteen words and could spell fifty words.

Now Raul's parents are teaching other parents how to listen to a child's world and how to thereby call forth all the potential locked in children who have been diagnosed as retarded or even autistic. They caution parents that not every child will respond as Raul did. But every parent can grow as he or she learns to listen and enter the child's world with unconditional love that says, "I love you as you are, and I feel what you are going through."

Listening to Ourselves

Compassion comes from the Latin *com*, meaning "with," and *pati*, meaning "to feel or suffer." To have compassion is to feel or suffer with another. When I listen compassionately to another, I feel within myself what his or her world is like, as Raul's mother felt his imprisonment in autism. When listening to another, I

---

2. Barry Kaufman, *Son Rise* (New York: Harper & Row, 1976).

also need to listen to myself because my thoughts and feelings may be internal clues that can help me understand what the other wants to communicate. Sometimes when I have difficulty listening to a person I want to get rid of the painful feelings I experience (frustration, boredom, emptiness, etc.), but these very feelings may be my clue to understanding that person's painful world.

I (Sheila) learned this several years ago when a friend, Bill, and I were praying on a weekly basis with a religious sister. Sr. Martha had many serious problems and was deeply depressed. Bill and I genuinely liked Sr. Martha, and outside of our prayer sessions we enjoyed her company. But during our prayer sessions, he and I would both experience increasing frustration as she went through her list of problems. I wished she would stop talking and get healed so I wouldn't have to keep listening to all this. By the time Sr. Martha would leave, we were glad to see her go and despairing that we were making any real progress. This went on for several months, while Sr. Martha seemed to grow worse and even attempted suicide.

One day it occurred to Bill and me that if we felt so much frustration in just listening to Sr. Martha's problems, how much more frustrated she must feel in having to live with them. And then we realized that perhaps Sr. Martha had no words adequate to convey the depth of frustration in her life, and perhaps her only way of inviting us into her world was to produce the same frustration in us.[3] During our following sessions with her, each time I felt irritated and frustrated with her list of problems, I would find a way to tell Sr. Martha that I knew she lived with inexpressible frustration in her life and that I wanted to be with her in her feelings. Bill did the same. Week by week I noticed how my own irritation and frustration were changing to compassion and patience. And during those weeks Sr. Martha began to get well. Her lifelong depression gradually lifted, and today she is a happy person who reaches out herself to pray for others. I think the turning point for Sr. Martha was that she finally felt someone had heard her cry of pain and communicated to her that she was no longer alone.

Sometimes, as in the case of Raul's mother or of Sheila praying with Sr. Martha, the feelings of frustration and despair they felt were an internal clue to the frustration and despair that Raul and Sr. Martha wanted to communicate. But at other times when I (Matt)

listen to my feelings I find that they are telling me about a block within myself that prevents me from listening to another. The block may be stress in the present moment. For example, when I receive three demanding phone calls in a row I find myself exhausted and unable to listen to anyone else. My feelings of exhaustion are telling me that I need help before I will be able to help another, and in such situations I am often helped by making a phone call to a friend who will listen to my needs. I can listen best to another when I am peaceful and have had my own needs listened to.

But what do I do when I'm not under stress and still find I can't listen compassionately to another, and perhaps even dislike that person? If I listen to myself, I will usually find that I am blocked in listening to that person because I am running either from what I have found in another that I don't like in myself, or from the pain of a past hurt.

To find out if my difficulty in listening is because I am running from the pain of a past hurt, I can ask Jesus, "When in the past did I most feel this way?" For instance, for a long time I couldn't listen to a lady who treated me like a canonized saint, always shouting my praises to any of her friends who would still listen. I tried to smile on the outside, but inside I was shouting back, "Let me be me and not a damn china statue on a stage." Then I remembered how I felt as a child when I was trotted around every year to recite my Christmas poem to a stuffy aunt who would slobber over me with praises while I wanted to get away and build a snowman or put a snowball through her window. As I healed that hurt with Jesus, I could again listen to my aunt and to the lady who sounded so much like her. When I can't listen, it is often because my hurt wants to say something back.

Sometimes when I (Dennis) can't listen, what I want to say is not, "I have been hurt," but rather, "I find in you what I don't like in myself." For instance, one day I realized that for over a month I had put off a phone call to confront Carol. Whenever Carol had a problem with me, she would call my provincial or my bishop rather than confront me first with what was on her mind. It was only when I was about to throw away her phone number that I realized I had the same problem I disliked in her. I didn't want to call Carol because, like her, I didn't like to confront another and tell that person what was on my mind. So I sat down with Jesus and saw the destruction that occurred when I didn't confront others. I also saw how Jesus loved me even in all the moments when I didn't confront people and how he wanted to empower me to confront with

---

3. Eugene Kennedy, *On Becoming a Counselor* (N.Y.: Seabury, 1977) pp. 18-32.

love. With each memory of failure to confront others, I breathed out my fears (e.g., fear of not being listened to, fear of disapproval) and breathed in Jesus' empowering love. After the prayer I called Carol and shared about how I had prayed for healing that morning. I even surprised myself when I asked her forgiveness for times I had not listened to her or had overreacted with disapproval. As I began to ask questions that helped Carol speak of her fears, I could respond and love her in the same way that Jesus had just loved that same part of myself. By the time Carol got around to answering why she kept calling my provincial, I was aware how easy it was to listen to her words (even though some of her words seemed to me like rationalizations).

Listening Together to Jesus

After listening compassionately to the other person and myself, then I can begin to listen prayerfully with the other to Jesus. I listen to Jesus not to find the right answer to a problem, but rather to get in touch with how much he loves the person with the problem and wants to fill him or her with his life. If the other person wants prayer, I begin by asking Jesus to reveal to us how he is with us and loves us. Then we remain silent so we can both sense how much he loves and wants to heal. I often just try to become Jesus loving the person as much as Jesus does with his mind and heart. When I feel Jesus taking over and loving the other person through me, then I am drawn into how he wants to begin and which of my ideas about how to pray are in tune with how Jesus wants to love that person. The deeper the love, the deeper I can discern the way of Jesus and not just the way of my wisdom.

The decision of how to pray should be shared with the other person, perhaps by asking "What have you heard as you listened? How do you think Jesus wants to begin?" Sometimes I may think I know a specific painful incident which has hurt the person and which Jesus wants to heal. For example, I might sense that the person as a teenager was sexually abused by her father. But even if I am right, the incident might be too painful for her to face yet. If it is difficult for her to face, I might say, "Do you remember any hurt with your father that occurred while you were a teenager? Shall we pray and see if Jesus brings any incident to your mind?" As I move gently and lovingly with a person and as I suggest general possibilities for how to pray, that person usually will begin to get in touch with painful incidents and share these in his or her own time and way. It is much more important and more healing to build a relationship of love, respect and trust with another person than it is to find "the answer."

But what if the person can't tell me anything and I have no idea of how to begin the prayer? That happened when someone asked me to pray for Louise, whom I had never previously met. Louise sat huddled in such psychic pain that she shook with fear and couldn't speak. I asked Jesus to show us how much he loved Louise. The more I loved her as Jesus, the more I sensed that she was being struck and Jesus wanted to love her as he did while being scourged at the pillar. It was so real that she began to shout, "Don't hit him!" Then Jesus showed her how he was holding not a pillar but her and taking into his body all the blows she received. She was shaking because she had been a battered child. As she let each blow strike Jesus protecting her, the shaking stopped. She watched Jesus choose to receive each blow so that he could forgive the one hitting him. Finally, she joined Jesus in forgiving her parents and began to experience deep peace. Louise had a history of psychiatric hospitalization. That day she turned a corner and began to make great strides in her therapy because she had traded hearts with Jesus—her battered heart for his forgiving heart. Today she works as a therapist, listening with compassion rooted in her own suffering and knowing that as she prays Jesus can do as much for another as he did for her.

Louise's story illustrates how the Spirit will help us pray even when we know nothing about the person. Although it is very important to listen to another and to ourselves, it is even more important to listen to the Spirit. Step by step the Spirit will guide us as the Spirit guided Jesus, if we can compassionately love as Jesus. The more we love as Jesus, the more we can listen to another, to ourselves, and to the Spirit of Jesus.

PRAYER FOR LISTENING TO JESUS

1. Join Mary Magdalene listening at the feet of Jesus (Lk 10:38–42).

2. Let Jesus help you recall the people in your life who have really listened to you and thereby empowered you to listen too. As you recall a name, breathe in and receive from Jesus the way that person loved you and empowered you to listen in the same way.

Chapter 6
Praying with Another

Once you have listened to someone seeking prayer, how do you begin praying as Jesus would pray? There are as many ways of praying with another as there are ways of loving. Prayers can range from a simple laying on of hands and letting the love of Jesus flow into the other in absolute silence, to prayers utilizing special gifts like the word of knowledge that reveals the specific incident such as a forgotten pre-natal trauma. While we should pray for these special gifts of the Spirit (e.g., tongues, prophecy, counsel, wisdom, etc.) that facilitate healing prayer, we should not conclude that only those with special gifts are called to healing prayer. The Lord wants to use everyone who can give Jesus' love even if the person can do no more than silently lay hands upon another and become Jesus' channel for healing love. Children can do little more than this, but their prayers are often more powerful than profound adult prayers.

A simple prayer for healing a hurt or burdened heart is the prayer of trading hearts with Jesus. Recently I (Matt) prayed with twenty-two-year-old Cindy. When Cindy was fifteen and feeling depressed, she took an overdose of drugs and ended up in a coma in an intensive care unit. From that time on, Cindy felt as if all the life were drained from her. She had little clarity of thought and constantly heard voices. Doctors classified Cindy as schizophrenic.

After listening to Cindy's story and getting in touch with Jesus' desire to make her whole, Cindy and I both prayed and asked Jesus, "When did you meet someone like Cindy? Where do you want to begin to heal her?" What came to both of us was the story of Jairus' daughter (Lk 8:49–56). In that story Jesus takes the hand of the little teenage girl who also had all the life drained from her, and then Jesus pours his strength into her body and calls her back to life. Jesus was inviting Cindy to be like Jairus' daughter so that he could give her strength in the midst of her coma and call her back to life.

After listening to Cindy, to my own reactions, and to Jesus so that I know how to pray, the second step is that of praying so as to meet Jesus and to trade hearts with him. Before someone like Cindy can face and share with Jesus the painful memory in her heart, she needs the strength that comes from knowing Jesus is present and filling her with his love. To help Cindy get in touch with Jesus' loving presence, I invited her to relax her body and place her hands in an open position so that her whole body was saying, "Lord, come. I'm open to you." With Cindy part of the relaxing process involved helping her shift her focus away from her fears and problems and toward Jesus. I asked Cindy to breathe out "fear" and breathe in the name "Jesus" until she began to experience Jesus' love filling her. If Cindy had not been able to get in touch with Jesus' love through this Breath Prayer, I might have asked her to remember her favorite time or favorite place (e.g. a spot down by a river or under a tree), or the time in her life when she felt most loved by Jesus—and then just rest in it.

After Cindy was centered in Jesus' loving presence, I read how Jesus healed Jairus' daughter (Lk 8:49–56) and invited Cindy to enter that scene in any way she could. First, I asked Cindy to focus on what she could see. Could she see Jesus enter the daughter's room? Then we focused on her sense of hearing. Could she hear Jesus' words, "Fear is useless. What is needed is trust," spoken with an authority to banish all fear? Finally, we focused on touch. Could Cindy imagine herself as the daughter lying in the corner of the room and feel Jesus' breath as he leaned over her, his hand taking her hand and his strength coming into her?

I asked Cindy to use her imagination to enter the scene in several different ways because some people are better able to pray with images, others with sounds, and still others with touch. Although Cindy could use her imagination in all three ways, touch was her easiest way to experience Jesus' love and let it fill her. When I asked her "What are you experiencing?" she said that she was being washed, as if a fountain of living water were flowing through Jesus' hand and swirling throughout her body, washing, cleansing and bringing her new life. Although she was using her imagination, it was not just her imagination but really Jesus touching her because she was taking on his mind and heart at the deepest levels opened by the imagination. According to legend, when Joan of Arc was accused of just imagining her visions, she replied, "Of course it's my imagination. How else would God speak to me?" She knew that after these imagined visions she loved God and others more and thus knew that what she imagined was what God wanted to communicate to her.

Different personality types communicate with God in different ways.[1] The sensate person (as in Mark's Gospel with its detailed stories) seeks to gaze with all his or her senses, simply contemplating Jesus present now and resting in that presence like a child resting in its mother's arms (Ps 131). The more intuitive person (as in John's Gospel) responds with the imagination to symbols and beauty, to prophecies of future dreams, and to the Gospel of hope. Thinkers (as in Matthew's Gospel) seek objective truths such as the Beatitudes, and through self-examination they try and root out all disorder opposed to Jesus as teacher. Feelers (as in Luke's Gospel) value relationships over objective truth and are drawn to the compassionate Jesus caring for the poor and weak as in the story of the prodigal son, the good Samaritan, or the grateful tenth leper. But just as each Gospel does not confine itself to one personality type in trying to describe various aspects of Jesus, so, too, in prayer we may be drawn to pray in a different way so as to meet all aspects of Jesus. Very often the way we have been hurt is the way Jesus chooses to meet and heal us. Those wounded by angry words often hear Jesus speaking truth to them, and rape victims defiled by touch are eventually embraced by Jesus. An awareness of how the many ways different personalities meet Jesus helps, not so that we can program their prayer, but so that we can encourage others to stay with Jesus in the way that is their way even if not our way.

When a person like Cindy is being filled with Jesus' life, I encourage her to stay there. Perhaps the most common error in healing prayer is to run too soon from being loved. A person receiving prayer may want to start praising God or promising to do things for him. The hardest and most healing step is often simply to rest and to receive more of Jesus' love which empowers us to love as we are being loved.

Cindy was able to receive Jesus' love by entering the scene of Jesus praying for Jairus' daughter. But if Cindy had difficulty receiving Jesus' love in that scene, I would have told her what I was seeing, hearing and feeling as I prayed, or perhaps even have chosen a different way to pray. But I do not want to take a person like Cindy into her painful memory until she experiences Jesus' presence and feels filled with his love.

During the first part of the prayer where Cindy experienced Jesus filling her with his love, I simply tried to be Jesus loving her with his mind and heart. As I found myself becoming Jesus, I tried to lay my hand on her shoulder, just as gently and lovingly as Jesus laid his hand on Jairus' daughter. Then I began to take Cindy's hand as Jesus did in the story, and I let Jesus' life flow through my hands and into Cindy. Jesus constantly used touch to channel his love with people that his culture forbade him to touch such as women, lepers, or the dead. If a person is open to it, as Cindy was, I find it helpful to pray for healing by laying hands on the person, in the same way that Jesus prayed and asked us to pray (Mk 16:18).

Both the Roman Catholic Church and the medical profession recognize the healing power of touch. In all the sacraments but one, the Roman Catholic Church invokes the healing power of the Spirit through the laying on of hands. Medical studies show that lack of touch can trigger illnesses such as marasmus in newborn babies, whereas loving touch can be one of the most effective ways to heal a person in a coma.[2] Dr. James Lynch in *The Broken Heart* tells of how burn patients monitored while in a near coma would record their healthiest readings whenever the nurse held their hand to take their pulse.[3] Loving human touch heals.

Frequently as I try to become Jesus, I find myself with no words and yet with Jesus' life flowing into the person mainly through touch. At other times, especially as touch moves me deeper into loving a person as

1. W. Harold Grant, Magdala Thompson, Thomas Clarke, *From Image to Likeness: A Jungian Path in the Gospel Journey* (New York: Paulist Press, 1983).

2. For an overview of the healing effects of touch, see Ashley Montagu, *Touch: The Human Significance of the Skin* (New York: Harper & Row, 1978).

3. James Lynch, *The Broken Heart* (N.Y.: Basic Books, 1979).

Jesus, I can begin to feel what Jesus wants to say. Especially at those times when the person's problem seems to be bigger than the Problem Solver, I might try to pray aloud the prayer I find in Jesus' heart or tell the person what Jesus seems to be saying to him or her. After holding Cindy's hand and letting Jesus' life flow through my hands and into her, I shared with her the words Jesus seemed to be telling her.

> You are special to me because of everything you have gone through. No other hand takes your place. Let me hold your hand as no one else ever has and no one else ever will be able to. You belong to me, and I won't let go of you, forever. There is nothing you face that I can't walk through with you.

But whether or not I pray with another by using the laying on of hands, or by using words, I try to be Jesus, loving the person in the ways Jesus wants to love him or her. Praying with another does not require extraordinary gifts such as words of knowledge or visions (although these can be very helpful). It requires only that I be Jesus and love with Jesus' love. If I am not sure how Jesus wants to love another, I can simply ask, "What are you experiencing?" Then I encourage the person to keep returning to whatever ways Jesus is loving or was lovingly experienced before any distraction came. Once a person is connected to Jesus, my role becomes less active as I simply underline whatever Jesus is doing and encourage the person to continue to receive Jesus' love.

After Cindy was filled with Jesus' love, she was ready to invite Jesus into her painful memory. She could do this because she continued to hold the hand of Jesus. This not only allowed her to keep drawing in love, but also to pull in from Jesus everything she needed such as his clarity of thought, his strength of body, and his courage that can even turn people from drugs and give them new life again. As Cindy returned with Jesus to the time when she overdosed in a suicide attempt and ended up in a coma, she began to feel depressed.

We have already mentioned the five stages, such as the stage of depression Cindy experienced, involved in healing a memory and how to watch what Jesus says and does in each stage (Chapter 3). As Cindy held my hand tightly it seemed that all Jesus wanted to say or do was what he had done earlier. So, two or three times when it appeared as if Cindy might get lost in her pain, I invited her to return to her experience of consolation (Chapter 4) and again feel Jesus' strong hand or his living waters cleansing and bringing new life.

There is a balance between focusing on the pain of a memory and focusing on Jesus' love. Getting in touch with pain is good only to the extent that it leads us to hold on to Jesus' hand tighter. If a person denies all pain, he or she will not be hungry for Jesus' healing love. But if a person focuses too much on the pain, he or she may begin to despair. In that case, the person should focus less on pain and more on Jesus' love. Healing begins when someone like Cindy feels God's love in the midst of the pain. As Cindy told us at the end of the prayer, the most healing time for her was when she had taken Jesus into the depth of her pain. At that moment, Cindy heard Jesus say to her that she was special to him because of everything they had been through together, and that he would never let go of her hand.

After Cindy knew how special she was to Jesus, she could return with him to the suicidal feelings, the overdose and the coma without becoming depressed. I asked her again the simple question, "What are you experiencing, Cindy?"

> Cindy: That Jesus is proclaiming something.
> Matt: Just watch what he's proclaiming.
> Cindy: He's proclaiming that I'm going to be okay. I'm holding on to Jesus' hand and he's picking me up off the ground as though I'm soaring with him.

So Cindy, even in the midst of her most painful memory, felt like Jairus' daughter as Jesus took her hand and picked her up while filling her with his risen life.

As we continued to pray, Cindy kept experiencing risen life coming into what was a painful memory. When she recalled the painful memory of her suicide attempt, she described not the pain but how Jesus was lovingly present holding her hand. When no more pain is surfacing and a person is getting deeper and deeper into Jesus' love, then we can start to bring the prayer to a close and begin thanking God for whatever has happened. The gratitude will be spontaneous and not forced if the person's hurt has begun to heal, bringing him or her into the acceptance stage, marked by power to reach out and gratitude (Chapter 3). So we each said heartfelt thanks to the Lord and then after the prayer shared with each other why we were grateful.

The important thing in prayer is not how much happened, but rather how grateful we are for whatever has happened and how eager we are to meet the Lord again and love him even more. When a child gives a dandelion to his or her mother, what matters is not the value of the gift but the love with which it is given. In prayer, what matters is not whether we had great feelings or moving experiences. What matters in prayer is that whatever we received came from a hand that really loves us. The more we can respond to whatever is given us in prayer and see it as precious because it is given with love, the more we build up our relationship with God and become eager to love him more. We become like the mother who in receiving a dandelion as a precious gift has built up her relationship with her child and becomes eager to love that child even more.

BREATH PRAYER

(For gratefully centering oneself in Jesus' love.)

1. Sit erect, feet flat on the floor, hands on your lap, palms up without touching each other. Become aware of the openness of your hands and the air at your fingertips, between your fingers, and on your palms.

2. Take a deep breath, as if you were breathing through your toes, and let that breath be carried up through your legs, abdominal muscles, lungs—your entire body. As you breathe in, say silently, "Lord Jesus Christ," while taking in whatever you need from him: his peace, joy, risen sexuality, wisdom, etc. You may want to visualize Jesus standing before you or see him looking into your eyes. See his body of light and experience that light coming into your own body as you inhale his presence.

3. Check your body for any tension. Release the tension by tensing up a given muscle and then relaxing it or by rotating your jaw or other joint. As you exhale, smile and breathe out whatever may have been that tension. With each exhalation, surrender more deeply until you hunger for Jesus as much as you hunger for air.

Chapter 7
Follow-Up After Healing Prayer

Why after a great prayer session or retreat are we often in the same sad shape as we were in before? Perhaps because we pray well but follow up poorly. How can we best follow up a religious experience? A worried woman with two notebooks full of workshop notes, names of people she needed to forgive, and resolutions she was going to work on asked Agnes Sanford, "What's the most important thing for me to do after this retreat?" After glancing through the notebooks, the lists of people to forgive, and the resolutions to work on, Agnes looked at the woman and asked, "What way do you most enjoy receiving love that gives you life?" Then Agnes said, "When I finish a retreat, what I enjoy is going home and digging in my garden."

Receiving Love

Perhaps the biggest mistake in follow-up, whether of a workshop or of a prayer experience, is that people become work-oriented, wondering what they should *do*. But follow-up (which is as necessary for the person praying as the person prayed for) begins not with doing but with enjoying the ways you can receive love. Some can receive love not so much through gardening as through jogging, dieting or the beauty of a work of art or music. One of my favorite ways of receiving love is to cook a Chinese meal (with all its colors, tastes and textures) and share it with my friends. An important question for follow-up besides "What way do you most enjoy receiving love from God who gives you new life?" is "Who are your friends and what way do you most enjoy receiving God's love from them?" A person will continue to grow if they have one significant person to enjoy and share life with.

Perhaps the factor that most determines whether people will continue to grow or not is: Do they have at least one friend with whom they can share how they are growing or struggling and then with whom they can pray in order to invite Jesus to be there? Thus when people come for prayer, I usually have them bring a friend who can continue to do this follow-up. One marriage counselor simply teaches the husband and wife to pray together in silence. The husband asks his wife how she wants prayer and then spends five minutes or so just laying his hand upon her and filling her with Jesus' love. Then they reverse roles. The counselor finds that if they can do this simple prayer with each other, their love for each other becomes alive again and their problems assume solvable proportions.

Some people may feel the need for a more structured setting in which to meet such a friend, so I might suggest a support group such as Al-Anon, Alcoholics Anonymous, groups for the divorced or widowed, or perhaps a prayer group. For a few, whose emotional stability continues to deteriorate, I also have the responsibility to encourage them to seek professional help. (Possible signs of a need for professional help are: inability to sleep, eat, deal with recurring suicidal thoughts or continue with one's ordinary work.) For others, I might suggest that they seek outside help because of a problem in myself. For instance, I may be unable to help them face grief because I have not been able to grieve a loss in my own life. But if both of us are growing from sharing together, then the similar problem can create compassion. In Alcoholics Anonymous, for example, an alcoholic who is still very ill will only become more ill by trying to help others too soon. But if an alcoholic is substantially recovered, then reaching out to help other alcoholics will bring even more new life and healing to both helper and client. Jesus' favorite healers are often wounded healers.

Some receiving prayer may be so wounded that they become very dependent, even calling me to check out each move they are going to make. If I think they are people for whom dependency on me will not bring growth, I usually ask them, "What do you hear Jesus saying in prayer as you ask him what you have asked me?" I then encourage the ways they are being guided by Jesus or tell them to pray about it, so that the main focus is on relating to Jesus, not me. With others who suffer from deprivation neurosis and have never trusted or been unconditionally loved by another, this dependency on me may be a temporary, normal, healthy part of their growth and development. Such people will naturally move through their dependency at their own pace as they are gradually strengthened by my affirming love. I may still set limits on phone calls, etc. because of my own needs, but I accept their need to be dependent upon me. As they recognize that I will be faithful, they can risk further trusting themselves, new friends and Jesus.[1]

Such loving and trusting friendships will be the key for Cindy's (see Chapter 6) growth and development which, through drug and suicidal traumas, became arrested at adolescence, an important period of her growth and development. Since without love human beings cannot grow or develop normally, the hurts surrounding her suicide attempt at age fifteen left Cindy not only with many unloving memories and people to forgive, but also with arrested growth in the adolescent stage of her life. Sometimes people like Cindy may need to grow up all over again, and I may feel impatient, like a mother who is anxious for her child to stop creeping and begin walking.

But behavior that appears childish to us may actually be a sign of growth and new health. For example, a friend of ours, George, was never touched or held as a child. Not only did he suffer the hurt of feeling deprived and lonely throughout his childhood, but George also never grew up emotionally. Even as a 6'2" thirty-five-year-old man, he remained a small child within. George received prayer and counseling for his early hurts, but his healing was not complete until he relived the stages of childhood development he had missed. His therapist understood George's need to

---

1. Affirming love may include loving guidance if given at the right time and in the right way. For a beautiful and simple treatment of the meaning of affirmation, see Conrad W. Baars, M.D., *Born Only Once: The Miracle of Affirmation* (Chicago: Franciscan Herald Press, 1975). For a complete discussion of the symptoms and treatment of the seriously unaffirmed or deprivation neurotic person, see Conrad W. Baars, M.D. and Anna A. Terruwe, M.D., *Healing the Unaffirmed* (New York: Alba House, 1976). For a discussion of healthy dependency and healing prayer, and specifically the dangers of interrupting a healthy dependency, see Conrad W. Baars, M.D., "When the Power To Heal Becomes Destructive," *Journal of Christian Healing*, Vol. 5, No. 1, Spring 1983, pp. 3–9.

grow up all over again, and gave George the fatherly love he had never received. With his therapist's encouragement, George began to spend time playing in a sandbox, enjoying childish play for the first time in his life. He did this until he no longer felt the desire for it. For George, what appeared to be a regression to childhood was really a sign of growth and healing because it opened him to enjoying life and to giving and receiving love. Follow-up prayer for him meant asking Jesus each day, "How old am I today, and how do you want to love me so I can continue growing up?"

For those as wounded as George or Cindy, follow-up prayer should also be a time of sharing, enjoying life and deepening the healing we have received rather than opening up new hurts. A wise psychiatric nurse tells people after she has prayed with them: open up no new hurts in prayer for the next several weeks. So after praying with Cindy, I (Matt) suggested that she continue in prayer to receive love into the hurt of her suicide attempt, in order to continue changing her habit of suicidal desires and to accomplish the growth that had been blocked by years of living with a deep hurt.

Because Cindy had lived with habits of suicidal desires and feelings of rejection for so long, these desires and feelings might surface again. Generally the first to change are our thought patterns and our actions, and finally our feelings. Perhaps she would still even hear voices and feel depressed after our prayer. Healing prayer doesn't necessarily take away the problem completely, but rather gives the person new freedom to choose. For instance, if her suicidal desires and feelings of rejection recurred, Cindy could return as before to her moment of consolation. Rather than choosing death, she could again hold tight to Jesus' hand and allow herself to be washed by the fountain of living water flowing through Jesus' hand and swirling throughout her body, washing, cleansing and bringing her life. She could recall Jesus tenderly telling her that she was special and that he would never let go of her hand. These words would daily reconstruct her self-image as loved and wanted rather than as rejected. Whether or not the voices or suicidal desires returned, I encouraged her to return to these moments of consolation daily—and if possible to have someone pray with her for a few minutes (even in absolute silence) so she could actually hold a hand and receive from it Jesus' love.

Sometimes the way to receive love is by going to Eucharist, reading Scripture, journaling, etc. These and other devotions are healing for the wounded to the extent that they help a person to receive love rather than call them to give love they cannot yet give. Frequently we suggest that a person center such devotions around celebration and gratitude—e.g., by asking "For what am I grateful today?" or "How has Jesus deepened the healing in me today?" But whether the person gardens, shares with a friend, or prays, the question is the same: "What way can you most enjoy receiving love that gives you new life?"

Giving Love

Once I am receiving love then I, like the woman at Agnes Sanford's retreat, can look at my notebook and ask the second question, "What should I *do* to give love?" Maybe I am called to eliminate compromises and adopt new disciplines. If I *do* without first receiving love I will usually be doing it because I *should* rather than because I *want,* and the result is usually more unrealistic goals and burnout. Ignatius says that the way the evil spirit will most frequently tempt good people is to over-extension and finally burn-out. I will know that it was the right time to do something if, after doing it, I feel more full of life (more able to give and receive love) than before. If I am not more full of life, then I probably reached out too soon, without first receiving enough love.

After having shared these thoughts with Cindy about how to receive love and give thanks for new life, I walked with her to the car. As I was walking back to the house, I wondered: Will her thinking clear? Will the voices disappear? What if the suicidal depression returns? What leads me to burn-out is needing everything to go perfectly or getting down on myself because I didn't pray the perfect prayer with the perfect results. The challenge for me is Mother Teresa's story.

A visitor once asked Mother Teresa, "How can you all day long keep constantly caring and praying for the dying or bathing lepers without burning out?" Mother Teresa said, "I have been called by the Lord not to be successful, but to be faithful." Frequently when praying with people I want to be successful. I want to pray and see results. I treat people as problems rather than as brothers and sisters whose pain I also feel. When I'm the Savior, looking forward only to how they will change, rather than leaving all the change up to Jesus and looking forward to being with them and loving them, then burn-out is probably around the corner. As I finished walking into the house, I felt more renewed as I breathed out all the ways I wanted Cindy to change and breathed in "Thanks" for all the ways Jesus had allowed us to enjoy giving and receiving love during our time together.

Once inside the house I prayed what I call the "Release Prayer." Releasing Cindy to Jesus' care was important because I could not continue to pray with Cindy due to geographic distance. But two months after my prayer with Cindy, I called and asked her what lasting changes she experienced as a result of our prayer together. She said that she has the greatest clarity of mind (the voices have almost completely disappeared) she has had in twenty-two years. Together with the clarity of mind, Cindy also felt more secure about herself and thus was able to go back to finish her high school education which she had put off for years.

Discovering the Release Prayer

I find deep life often comes to people like Cindy and myself when I pray the "Release Prayer." This prayer is important for me because after I lovingly pray with another, I can become a burden bearer wanting to do more for a person than I can do. At times like this I need to release the person and his or her problems into the hands of Jesus. One midnight Jesus taught me the power of physically releasing a problem into his hands. After a full day of workshops, I had just dragged myself into the chapel for a quick prayer before bed. I was so tired that I found myself dozing off as I tried to say just five words, "Thank you for this day." As I rose to go to my room, I heard a woman crying. I wanted to go to bed but realized that I would just lie awake wondering about her. So, in my own self-interest, I asked Joan if she wanted to talk.

For twenty minutes, Joan poured out her worries about her daughter: her daughter's husband drank and had run off leaving the bank ready to foreclose on their house, her sons were sick with fevers, the baby in her womb was in the wrong position for birth, etc. I told Joan that we couldn't do anything that night for her daughter, who lived five hundred miles away. I suggested that Joan just pray aloud, asking Jesus to care for her daughter and leaving her in Jesus' hands. So Joan prayed for another twenty minutes, telling Jesus all her worries over her daughter. But as soon as Joan ended the prayer, she began to cry again. Joan still held her daughter locked in a worried mother's heart.

I didn't know what to do next but in desperation (and my own need for sleep) I told Joan that we had to pray for her daughter again. I said to Joan, "You did well on describing the problem to Jesus but not so well on releasing the problem into his hands. This time, let's begin by cupping your hands, holding your daughter in them, and offering her to Jesus. Then pray again briefly, telling Jesus how your daughter needs his care. But this time release your daughter into Jesus' hands rather than take her back into your heart. Let Jesus, not yourself, worry about her tonight.''

Joan prayed for another full twenty minutes, squeezing her hands around her daughter and telling Jesus all her daughter's problems. Then Joan took a deep breath and opened wide her hands as she offered her daughter to Jesus. She no longer needed her own hands but was trusting the hands of Jesus to hold her daughter that night, with a love even greater than her own. After that prayer I was exhausted and grateful to finally get to bed.

The next afternoon, Joan came to find me, and I wondered what I would do next. But with a sparkle in her eyes, Joan shared, ''My daughter called this morning. During the night her husband came back home and he wants to go to Alcoholics Anonymous for help with his drinking. My two grandsons awoke with no fever. The bank called and can extend their loan. She even thinks her baby has repositioned itself for a normal delivery.'' I could hardly believe it, but five out of the daughter's eight problems had been solved that night as we simply released her out of our hands and into Jesus' hands.

Perhaps you too would like to release the person in your heart whom you worry about most. If so, the steps are very simple.

RELEASE PRAYER

1. Center on Jesus in any way you wish, perhaps by repeating ''Jesus'' as you breathe in and out (see end of Chapter 6).

2. Cup your hands and place in them a person you are concerned about.

3. Tell Jesus or the Father all that you long to have happen for that person. With each request, squeeze your hands more tightly as if you were squeezing into that person all that you long to give.

4. When you have said it all, open your hands and release the person into Jesus' hands.

5. Watch what Jesus says or does for the person. Be ready for surprises!

Chapter 8
The Healer in Healing

Sometimes I hear people who pray for healing say things like this: "When I pray for someone, I get myself completely out of the way and let Jesus do it all." Other times, I hear people say things like this: "Jesus uses our weaknesses. We can only help others in the ways we've been wounded ourselves." Or, "Jesus uses healed people. We can't heal others unless we've been healed ourselves."

When we pray for another, is it all dependent on Jesus, so that he does his work regardless of our weaknesses? Is it all dependent on us, so that our strengths and skills determine how much Jesus can do? Or is it both? And if it's both, what role do our weaknesses and our strengths play in the healing process?

God works through his creation, and so just as Scripture is both divinely inspired and the work of human authors,[1] so ministry is both dependent on Jesus *and* dependent on us. Jesus uses both our weaknesses and our strengths to the extent we have allowed them to be touched by his love. Paradoxically, sometimes our weakness makes us depend more on his strength which brings healing to another, while other times our weakness may cause us to be blind to the needs of another and project our own fears in ways that bring destruction to an already hurt person.[2] Our strengths may be gifts which empower us to heal, or they may be barriers to compassion, keeping us complacent in our self-sufficiency and unable to bring another the healing that comes from knowing he or she is not alone in needing a Savior.

How can I let both my weaknesses and my strengths be opportunities for Jesus to heal others

through me . . . and to continue healing me? I can begin by asking myself:

What does it mean

- when I want to run away from people with certain kinds of hurts?
- when I need people to change in certain ways?
- when I keep emphasizing the same thing in everyone I pray for?

The answers to these questions can tell me how I need to be loved by Jesus so I can be his love for others.

What Kinds of People Do I Run From?

When I (Sheila) ask myself what it means when I want to run away from people with certain kinds of hurts, I think of Linda. As mentioned in Linda's story in Chapter 3, Linda came to us for prayer because as a child she had been sexually abused by a relative. Although Linda had been in psychotherapy for fourteen years, she still felt anger at the relative who abused her, self-hatred because of her own subsequent sexual acting out, fear of being isolated from others whom she believed could never love her if they knew, and grief at the loss of her wholesome feminine identity. Thus Linda experienced a constant sense of inner emptiness and darkness.

Until recently, I ran away from people with the kind of hurt Linda had. I did this because I, too, was sexually abused as a child by a friend of my family. Although I reacted by withdrawing almost completely from men rather than by sexual acting out like Linda, I shared Linda's feelings of anger, fear and grief. When women who had been sexually abused came to me for prayer, their sharing recalled my own unhealed pain. I could not even listen to them without feeling frightened and depressed. I would find a way to change the subject or suggest they find someone else to help them.

1. Austin Flannery (ed.), *Vatican Council II: Conciliar and Post-Conciliar Documents*, (Northport: Costello, 1975), "Divine Revelation," III:11.

2. Conrad W. Baars, M.D., "When the Power To Heal Becomes Destructive," *op. cit.* William A. Barry and William J. Connolly, *The Practice of Spiritual Direction* (New York: Seabury, 1982), pp. 170–174.

If I had prayed with such a person during those years, I think she would have left with even more pain than when she arrived, having absorbed my raw emotions in addition to her own. When I want to run away from people with certain kinds of hurts, it's usually because they remind me of the same hurts in myself that I don't want to face.

A few years ago, the hurt of sexual abuse in my own life began to heal. Healing came through prayer, forgiveness of the person who abused me, spiritual direction and friendships with healthy men who loved me unselfishly. When Linda came to us and asked for prayer, I was able to listen to her story without fear or depression. Then I knew I was ready to join Dennis in praying with Linda.

Before Dennis and I prayed with Linda, I told her that I too had been sexually abused. This was healing for Linda and healing for me. It was healing for Linda because she knew she was not alone; she knew that I understood how she felt. My own healing deepened when I shared my experience with Linda because never before had I been able to share this with anyone except people who were praying with me, and then always with feelings of despair and embarrassment because I wanted this terrible hurt to be wiped out of my life. Now, for the first time, I saw how my experience could be a gift and source of life for another. I even felt grateful for what I had been through if it would help me to be present to Linda.

I saw my experience become a gift for Linda in two ways. First, from the time she originally came to us, I knew Jesus could heal her because I knew he had healed me. I knew Linda could have healthy relationships with men because I saw the new life and health in my own relationships with men. The hope and faith I felt for Linda during our first meeting rose spontaneously within me and never diminshed during the months that followed.

The second way my experience became a gift for Linda was in helping me know what she might need from Jesus and how Jesus might want to love her. At the beginning of our prayer with Linda, Dennis and I both had an expectation that Linda would forgive her relative. But Linda felt blocked in being able to forgive this person. As I tried to enter into how Jesus wanted to love Linda, I recalled how he had loved me. When people prayed with me for healing the hurt of sexual abuse, I learned that it was O.K. to be angry at the actions of the man who abused me and that Jesus loved me enough to be angry at that man's actions too. (Later, I saw Jesus' compassion for him.) I sensed that Jesus wanted to love Linda *with* her anger also, and even be angry on her behalf, rather than pushing her to forgive too soon. I thought of the scene where Jesus threw the money-changers out of the temple (Mt 21:12) and sensed that he felt the same anger over the temple of Linda's body. When I told Linda this, she had an image of Jesus coming into the temple and then yelling at the relative who had abused her. She began to cry with relief and gratitude that Jesus would love her enough to be angry for her. This was the first time in fourteen years of psychotherapy that Linda was able to cry. From that moment on, Linda's inner emptiness left her and has never returned. This is because she knows that Jesus is with her even in her anger and that "he wants to share all of me." The very feelings which previously had caused Linda to be isolated from others were now a way of her being united with Jesus. I was able to give up my expectation of what Linda *should* do and allow Linda to be angry without encouraging her to be vengeful (i.e., hate the sin and love the sinner) because of my own experience of how Jesus had loved me exactly as I was.

How Do I Need People To Change?

The second question I ask myself is: What does it mean when I need people to change in certain ways? At the beginning of Dennis' and my prayer with Linda, she felt blocked in her ability to forgive her relative. Near the end of our prayer, she felt blocked in her ability to forgive herself. We had asked Linda to enter into the scene of the woman caught in adultery and forgiven by Jesus (Jn 8:3–11). Linda saw herself as that woman and also saw herself as the person in the crowd who held the biggest stone. We tried in many ways to get Linda to put down her stone or give it to Jesus, but she was unable to do so. Finally, Dennis told Linda that she didn't have to give up her stone, that Jesus wanted to love her with the stone until she was ready to give it up. We saw the relief on Linda's face when Dennis said this. Later, she told us that the stone represented her sexuality. Even though Linda hated her sexuality, it was still hers . . . it was *her* stone. Linda said that she would never have trusted Jesus if he had forced her to give up her stone. She would have felt toward Jesus just as she had felt toward her relative who had forced her to give her sexuality.

At the beginning of our prayer, I had been more free to let Linda be as angry as she was, while Dennis was trying to get her to forgive. At the end of our prayer, I was trying to get her to change in certain ways while Dennis was more free to let her be as she was.

Why did I need Linda to change by giving up her stone before the end of our prayer?

I needed Linda to change for two reasons. First, when Dennis and I prayed with Linda it was only one year after I began working with Dennis and Matt, and it was the first time I had joined them in praying for someone on videotape. I knew Dennis' and Matt's reputation in the healing ministry, and especially their reputation for their work with forgiveness. People who didn't know us well but who had heard of Dennis and Matt would sometimes ask me, "Are you Dennis' and Matt's typist?" Each time I heard this, my first reaction would be anger at what seemed like an assumption based on clericalism and sexism . . . followed by wondering if I really was contributing anything of substance to their ministry. I wanted Linda to give up her stone and forgive herself as a result of my prayer with her so that I could be successful in the eyes of myself, of Dennis and Matt, and of anyone else who might think I was just "Dennis' and Matt's typist."

When Dennis told Linda that she could keep her stone, I shared Linda's relief. I realized I didn't have to be "successful" in praying with Linda any more than Linda had to be "successful" in forgiving herself. I knew that just as Jesus, Dennis and I cared more about Linda than about whether she forgave herself or not, so Jesus, Dennis and Matt cared more about me than whether I was "successful" in praying a "perfect" prayer.

The second reason I needed Linda to change by giving up her stone was because I am frightened by lasting, unresolved conflict. I could let Linda be angry at her relative and know that Jesus was with her in her anger, but I didn't want Linda to go away angry at her relative or at herself. I can accept anger in myself or in others, but I want it to get worked out. Over the next months, as I was able to stay with Linda in her anger at herself, my fear of lasting, unresolved conflict began to diminish. When I need a person to change in certain ways, it's usually because I need to be successful or because something about where that person is frightens me.[3]

What Do I Keep Emphasizing in Everyone I Pray For?

The third question I ask myself is: What does it mean when I keep emphasizing the same thing in everyone I pray for? Matt sometimes teases me that I treat everyone as if they were in the second week of the *Spir-*

 itual Exercises, while he treats everyone as if they were in the first week. (The *Spiritual Exercises of St. Ignatius* is a four-week retreat process commonly used by Jesuit retreat directors. The "weeks" need not be understood literally, so that a person might be in the first "week" throughout a thirty-day retreat. Persons in the first week are not yet centered on the Lord and may be attracted by evil and repelled by good, while persons in the second week are centered on the Lord and usually repelled by evil and attracted by good.) The truth of Matt's teasing is that, while he tends to see the ways people still need to grow, I tend to see everyone and everything as good.

I assume that if I give people enough authentic love and enough time, they will naturally grow and make good choices. I assume this because my experience of myself is that when I am given enough authentic love and enough time, I naturally grow and make good choices. I have so much internal pressure to grow and to do what is right that when external pressure is added, the weight is too much and I become paralyzed and stuck. I was over-disciplined as a child, and received frequent criticism from several authority figures. I am still very sensitive to criticism and easily discouraged by it, whereas I flourish in an atmosphere of trust and praise. In such an atmosphere I can let myself be, and I can release some of the pressure to grow and do everything right. When I pray with another, I want to give them what I myself need because I assume they are like me. When I keep emphasizing the same thing in everyone I pray for, e.g., the need to be free of pressure to grow and to do everything right and the need for trust and praise, it's because that's what I am most in need of myself.

The gift in what I emphasize is that I am quick to see the good in others and thus able to draw it out, since people do tend to become what others see in them. I can also be very patient with their process of growth and "let them be" for a long time. The danger in what I emphasize is that I may be blind to moments when evil affecting a person needs to be confronted rather than "let be," or to the type of person who, unlike myself, needs more structure rather than less.

During the months after Dennis and I prayed with Linda, she began coming to a friend, Sr. Marie, and me for prayer on a weekly basis. Although Linda's inner emptiness was gone, she still felt considerable darkness and was unable to forgive herself for her own sexual acting out. During these months, I treated Linda as I would have wanted to be treated. I kept seeing the good in her and drawing it out. Although Linda began calling Sr. Marie and me every day to ask for reassur-

3. Frank Lake, *Tight Corners in Pastoral Counseling* (London: Darton, Longman and Todd, 1981), Chapter 12.

ance, I never lost patience with her. I assumed that if I just continued to love and affirm Linda, she would grow and be healed.

To a certain extent, my assumption was right. Linda grew to trust me deeply, the first time she had ever trusted a woman. Linda felt safe with me, knowing that I saw her as good and that I would not abandon her, no matter how often she asked for reassurance. With many people my approach would have been enough, and confrontation or pressure to grow would have been harmful.[4] With Linda, however, my tendency to see everything as good made me slow to recognize her need for deliverance ministry.[5] Linda remained stuck in her ability to give up her stone of self-hatred and continued to experience deep inner darkness. Sr. Marie was quicker than I to see that we needed to take an active stand against the evil forces affecting Linda.

During the next several weeks, my gift of building Linda up in love and Sr. Marie's gift of sensing the presence of evil spirits worked together. Finally we had a Eucharist for Linda and her family in which we prayed in Jesus' name for deliverance from spirits of self-condemnation, incest and sadistic sexual violence. The day after the Mass Linda called to tell us that her inner darkness was gone and she felt happy for the first time in her life. The inner darkness has never returned and today she reports a constant sense of inner peace and well-being, even in times of difficulty.

I had led Linda in a prayer renouncing the evil spirits. As I looked back later on this moment, I realized that not only Linda but I too was healed as I stood by her and stood up to evil. Although unlike Linda I had not needed deliverance prayer during the time when I was receiving ministry, my ability to confront evil had been hampered by my childhood experience of sexual abuse. Like many girls who have been sexually abused by an adult world which is supposed to protect them, I was left with an impaired capacity to protect myself, a fearfulness and lack of confidence in my ability—and even my right—to resist that which might harm me. I tended to turn anger, hatred and assertiveness in upon myself, hesitant to use the energy of these emotions as it was intended, to fight evil and obtain what is good.[6]

Soon after our Eucharist with Linda, I went to the east coast, where I grew up, to visit the person who had abused me. Although I had forgiven him to the extent of feeling compassion rather than anger when I thought of him, and had even grown to see ways that my experience had become a gift, I did not think I could ever have a real relationship with this man or that his life could ever change. When I visited him, I saw the circumstances in his life that had caused his disturbed behavior toward me. Everyone in his family had given him up for dead, believing that these circumstances could not be changed. I realized that it was not so much he who had oppressed me, but the destructive forces in his life that had oppressed both of us, and I began to fight against these forces to save his life.

I organized his family members and professional helpers to reach out to him. I knew there was little chance of success after he had lived in darkness for so many years. Yet I found myself able to risk not being successful, perhaps because I had been able to give up my need to be successful with Linda. Other persons in this man's life became very angry at me for interfering in his situation, but I was able to risk their ongoing, unresolved anger just as I had become able to risk Linda's unresolved anger. Because I had faced and stood up to evil with Linda, I now found myself able to see clearly and fight the forces of evil in this man's life, harnessing all my energy of anger and hatred of evil and of assertiveness. What had been a passive sort of forgiveness of this person, where I just wished him well, now became an active giving-for as I worked to free him. He changed dramatically in response to feeling loved and supported for the first time in his life, and is now an emotionally healthy and happy person, living in a new and healthy environment. And I have a new and healthy relationship with him—a gift to both of us from Linda. Healing prayer even heals the healer.

PRAYER FOR HEALING THE HEALER

1. Ask Jesus to show you the person it is hardest to listen to or pray with.

2. Share with Jesus what you would like changed in that person or what feelings and struggles in that person you run from.

3. Let Jesus show you when you had similar feelings and struggles.

4. Breathe in the way Jesus loves you and wants to be present for you in the midst of those feelings and struggles.

---

4. Conrad W. Baars, M.D., "When the Power To Heal Becomes Destructive," op. cit.

5. Dennis and Matthew Linn, Deliverance Prayer, op. cit.

6. Conrad W. Baars, M.D., Feeling and Healing Your Emotions, op. cit.

Chapter 9
The Greatest Healing

As we travel the world, many ask us, "What is the greatest healing you have seen?" At first I shared stories of the blind seeing, the lame walking, and the poor shedding depressions and alcoholism as the Gospel is preached to them. But Jesus told a different story about the greatest healing.

> On his journey to Jerusalem he passed along the borders of Samaria and Galilee. As he was entering a village, ten lepers met him. Keeping their distance, they raised their voices and said, "Jesus, Master, have pity on us!" When he saw them, he responded, "Go and show yourselves to the priests." On their way there they were cured. One of them, realizing that he had been cured, came back praising God in a loud voice. He threw himself on his face at the feet of Jesus and spoke his praises. This man was a Samaritan.
>
> Jesus took the occasion to say, "Were not all ten made whole? Where are the other nine? Was there no one to return and give thanks to God except this foreigner?" He said to the man, "Stand up and go your way; your faith has been your salvation" (Lk 17:11–19).

Why was this the greatest healing? For the Jewish people, leprosy was the most dreaded of all diseases. A person who was blind or lame could continue to live with his family but a leper was cast out and no one could approach closer than one hundred and fifty feet if the wind was coming from the leper's direction. Although many skin diseases were considered as leprosy, for true leprosy the Jews had no treatment and it therefore meant certain death. Even in medieval times a leper was given a death certificate and had no rights or property, being treated as if dead. But a Jewish leper died rejected not only by people but also by God because his or her uncleanness was an obvious repudiation by God. Even if he or she touched others, they became unclean and sinners rejected by God. A rabbi was praised for his holiness because he refused to walk down a street used by a leper. There was no greater

healing than that of a leper because it meant restoring life to someone who had died rejected by humanity and by God. Leprosy was the greatest healing, and this was the greatest healing story because Jesus healed not one but ten lepers.

But Jesus shocks his Jewish audience by proclaiming an even greater healing. He points to the grateful Samaritan leper and says, "Was there no one to return and give thanks to God except this foreigner? Stand up and go your way; your faith has saved you" (Lk 17:18–19). "Saved you" is *sozo*, meaning a healing of the whole person—body, mind, and spirit. *Sozo* stresses the relationship with God whereas the other nine lepers are merely "purified" (*katharizo*). The greatest healing is to be grateful to God and to bring others to him as the leper did by his grateful praise. A gratitude that reaches out in love to God and others is the sign of the deepest healing.

When those who were sick return to give thanks by reaching out to others, entire communities are healed. Last year we visited Fr. Rick Thomas at Our Lady's Youth Center in El Paso, Texas. When we visited them, we found that nearly all the members had been healed in prayer and were now using their healing to reach out to others like themselves. For instance, many of his members praying now with prisoners or with delinquent youth had themselves been prisoners or delinquent youth and had gained freedom from drugs or self-hatred through healing prayer. Having been treated as outcasts for so long also gave them a compassion to reach out to the outcasts in mental hospitals. After they began to pray with the mental hospital patients, they found that in three weeks the bed patients were walking, in six weeks many were discharged as sane, and in three years only two out of the original patients remained hospitalized.

Their reaching out did not stop with prayer, but rather they reached out to build a better environment so that people could sustain their healing. Thus their community members also began a ranch to raise food for the poor and a labor union to unite warring factions of the garbage dump pickers. So much community building and healing was happening as wounded people became healed and then returned to heal others that Fr. Rene Laurentin came from Europe to document the happenings in *Miracles in El Paso?*

Many times I want to reach out to others as did the people in El Paso and yet I am frightened to do so. I often fear in the wounded person the struggles that are in myself. But this means that the person I most fear to touch with compassionate love is often the person who can best heal my wounds. For example, I (Matt) visited Carl, a priest who after heart surgery was left paralyzed, unable to speak and confused. Carl wanted to die, yet feared death. His fear affected me so much that I stayed in his hospital room only three minutes and even then nervously paced around and talked about his flowers as a distraction. I could not stay in his room because he was dying the very death I feared—paralyzed, confused, unable to speak and seemingly abandoned by a God who wasn't helping him to get better or to die.

Some weeks later during a retreat when nothing worked in my prayer, I experienced feeling paralyzed, confused, unable to speak a heartfelt prayer, and seemingly abandoned by God. Like the paralyzed priest, I struggled to be in control but finally had to simply let God love me in my poverty when I could do nothing for him. I was letting his healing love touch the deepest part of me that feared not just losing him in prayer but losing him at death if it was as terrifying as Carl's. In the middle of my retreat, I again visited Carl. This time my prayer had healed me enough to spend an hour compassionately loving Carl. But I still feared his death and sensed that Carl did too. So I took Carl's paralyzed hand and let it draw me into the fear I wanted to deny. With the other hand I held the hand of Jesus and prayed through the seven last words by which Jesus surrendered to a death much like Carl's which was so tangible and frightening. As we prayed, Jesus' love for us became deeper than our fear of death, and slowly we both could pass through our fear by surrendering to whatever life or death the Father might have for us. I realized that even if Carl because of his agony would denounce God, I would still love Carl and be with him and God would do no less. At my death too, the Father will be there for me even if I am not there for him. The next day Carl became more ill and within three weeks he was in the hands of the Father to whom he had en-

trusted his spirit. But Carl had also healed my deepest fear, and I can again be with the dying because Carl had been with me.

Whether in the case of myself and Carl, or of Fr. Rick Thomas bringing ex-prisoners back to minister in the prison, or of Sheila praying with Linda (see Chapter 8), our healing deepens as we return to heal others. One wise A.A. counselor told me that he can spot a reformed alcoholic who is about to start drinking again. His secret? He watches for a person who is no longer compassionately using his wounds to reach out to another alcoholic. Our very wounds if healed enough give us the compassion to reach out with love, and that very act further heals our wounds.

Usually the most powerful healing ministries will be in communities such as that of Fr. Rick Thomas in El Paso or in Alcoholics Anonymous where a conscious effort is made to reach out to the poor and broken. Isaiah 58:5–9 tells us to expect powerful healings where the homeless are sheltered, the hungry are fed and the works of mercy are celebrated. For instance, in India we asked what community had the most powerful healing ministry. Throughout India people said that the Poona prayer community attracted the sick because there were so many physical and emotional healings. One psychiatrist even sent his patients there and then became part of a healing prayer team. When we asked the leaders from Poona when this began, they said that little healing happened until they asked the Lord in prayer what he wanted them to do. Several people thought that the Lord was asking them to put two tables in the back of the room on which anyone who was healed would place gratefully a gift for the poor. Since the tables were set up, they have always been full because the Lord poured out his healing Spirit upon the community. Since there are many poor people in the prayer community, the leaders tell everyone that they can take from the tables whatever they need.

But no table can sufficiently meet all the needs of the poor, so the Lord empowers us through healing prayer to do even more. In Mexico we visited a leper colony where one woman who had been miraculously healed of cancer began to work as a way of expressing her gratitude. She found the lepers living in fear of being robbed or hurt by other lepers who had been rejected and hurt even by their own families. Since their greatest need was to form community and bonds of trust, she and a handful of her friends began a prayer meeting. Attracted by the singing, the lepers came and soon learned to receive love and reach out to each other in prayer.

As they laid their hands on a leper's broken body in prayer, the women began to compassionately feel the leper's painful world and Jesus' total love for each one. The women responded by bringing food, clothing, and medicine. But they could not meet the needs of three hundred lepers. So they taught the lepers how to help themselves by providing garden tools, sewing machines, and many hours of patient instruction—still too little for so many in need.

As the women searched for a way to do more, they found that the Mexican government had ten million pesos set aside for the care of lepers throughout Mexico, but only one million actually reached the lepers. They exposed this injustice by telling their husbands who told others until the government felt pressure from many people. Gradually the embarrassed government officials corrected the abuse and all ten million pesos again flowed to help lepers throughout Mexico. Thus a social structure was changed to help lepers throughout Mexico. And how? By a handful of ordinary women, all moved by compassion to lay their hands on and pray for one leper's broken body, until, feeling the leper's pain, they were moved to do more and more. Healing prayer begins by healing one person but ends by healing a nation.

Who empowered these ordinary women to keep reaching out? There were many but one was a grateful leper. Manuel has only stumps for hands but he uses the little he has to grow daisies. He digs the furrow with his foot, drops the seeds in from his mouth, and daily waters his flowers with a bucket in the crook of his elbow. Manuel gives his flowers away to the discouraged who need life or in gratitude to those who visit and bring life. When I arrived with the women, Manuel gave us each some flowers. They were ordinary flowers but they became priceless, offered between his stump hands that could do so little but that with the little loved so much. I had tears in my eyes as I took the flowers from his stumps. Manuel gave me not just flowers but the conviction that the Lord needs not great talents but the grateful leper's talent of great love.

THE TENTH LEPER'S PRAYER

1. Begin by praising and thanking Jesus for all he has done—especially the ways he has healed you in body, mind and spirit.

2. Recall Jesus' words, ''Whatever you do to the least of my brothers, you do unto me'' (Mt 25:40). With the love and gratitude you feel, reach out to another who is in need.

Chapter 10
Power to Heal

Perhaps after nine chapters, praying with another for healing seems very complicated. If you read a book on how to breathe, it could also seem very complicated. Fortunately, Jesus has given us an innate sense of how to breathe and of how to pray for another. He promised that his Spirit would guide us when we could not pray.

> The Spirit too helps us in our weakness, for we do not know how to pray as we ought; but the Spirit himself makes intercession for us with groanings that cannot be expressed in speech. He who searches hearts knows what the Spirit means, for the Spirit intercedes for the saints as God himself wills (Rom 8:26–27).

Learning to pray for healing is then not learning a method but learning how to listen to the Spirit who heals and knows every shortcut. Profound healing occurs when we give up on our own methods and search for the Spirit's way.

I learned how I have to listen more to the Spirit and less to my methods when I was in India praying for physical healing with Francis MacNutt and Barbara Shlemon, who have well-known healing ministries. A bishop came asking for prayer, and since the others were busy, another priest and I had the bishop all to ourselves. I thought, "This is great! I'll pray for this bishop and he will get healed. Then he will tell his priests that healing is real and parishes will come alive all over India." The bishop had a heart problem causing swelling in his legs. So I began to pray for the swelling in his legs to go down. I prayed for a few minutes but there was no change. I kept praying, trying every way I knew, even asking the bishop if he needed to forgive anyone. But nothing seemed to help. The bishop was in the same bad shape at the end as when we began, perhaps even worse, because of all I was going through. Finally I stopped and sat down exhausted. I

felt useless and wondered if some block in me was keeping the Lord's love from working through me.

While I was sitting down and feeling useless, two men carried in a twenty-eight-year-old woman named Pauline D'Sousa. About six months before, she had been in a train wreck outside of Bombay. In that wreck all her accompanying friends had died while yelling for help. In fact, of the sixty passengers, she was the only survivor on her train car. It had taken three hours to remove passengers from the wreckage and, in the process, a blow torch had cut through the nerves in Pauline's knee. Since then, Pauline had no sensation in her right leg below the knee. Thus she could not walk normally and had to wear special shoes with braces. The accident had also wrenched her back, and so she was in constant pain even with her back brace. In addition, she was depressed and unable to sleep because she constantly heard the two trains crunching together and her friends screaming for help. Pauline had tried many doctors since the train wreck, but none could help her any further.

I ignored Pauline because I was still feeling discouraged after praying with the bishop. I also thought that because of the severity of her injury, Pauline would need some special people like Barbara or Francis to pray for her. But they were still busy, and so a couple of us, including the bishop, decided to get started with Pauline until someone else could take over. When we met Pauline, we discovered that she couldn't speak English. So all my ideas of what inner healing prayer I could say to help heal Pauline's trauma were useless. All we could do was to try like Jesus to hold her and to love her. We prayed that way in total silence for about five minutes.

Then we asked her, through an interpreter, what she was experiencing. I had to ask her because I don't usually know exactly what God is doing. I've learned that I don't need dramatic words of knowledge to pray. All I need is Jesus' love. When I don't know what is happening, I just ask the person and then pray for more of whatever is happening to continue. Pauline said, "I felt as though Jesus was holding me. He came out of a bright light and for the first time in six months all my depression and anxiety are gone. I feel free." We had been praying for Jesus to hold her and to give her his peace. So we prayed for more peace. When we asked Pauline five minutes later what was happening, she said, "I feel as though my foot is buzzing. I'm beginning to have sensation in it." So we switched to praying for the right foot. After five minutes, she could move her big toe. Five more minutes of prayer, and she could move all her toes. After another five minutes, she could move her whole foot normally. We hadn't even thought of praying for Pauline's back, but that was healed too. In thirty minutes the Lord had healed her back, her foot, and all her depression. During the past five years none of Pauline's symptoms have returned.

We were amazed that so much healing happened to Pauline. But we should not have been amazed because the deepest healings Pauline experienced happen every time we pray with Jesus' compassion for the sick. Every time we pray, focusing not on techniques or results but on loving the sick as Jesus did, all involved in the prayer experience three things: first, more peace than before the prayer; second, a closer community than before; third, a deeper sense of being Jesus. The peace Pauline experienced was so deep that it permanently banished her depression and anxiety that drugs and therapy had not touched. Finally, the sense of community between us, even though we spoke different languages, was deeper than words could express. We knew in our hearts why Jesus wanted to call the woman with the flow of blood "daughter," the closest relationship possible (Lk 5:34). Then, too, when we prayed for Pauline, we knew what it meant to be Jesus, who spent two-thirds of his days allowing the Father's healing love to touch his sick children. Growth in peace, community and being Jesus are the deepest gifts given in healing prayer. They are always given when we focus on loving as Jesus and receiving his love.

Although these three gifts are always given, I had never seen so much physical healing happen as well. After praying with Pauline, I stood back and thought, "I don't understand this. Why, when I prayed with deep faith for the bishop, did no physical healing seem to happen? How come, when I prayed with hardly any faith for Pauline, she was healed?" I have thought of

two reasons which now help me to understand that strange evening. The first reason has to do with my attitude. When I was praying with the bishop, I was focused more on finding the right technique, since nothing worked. In contrast, when I was praying with Pauline, because she could not speak English, I could not use any techniques and had to focus on losing myself in Jesus and trying to be him for Pauline. In praying for Pauline, I had no faith in my prayer but only in Jesus' love. But the second reason why so much happened to Pauline was her attitude. Pauline was so confident of receiving Jesus' love that she had come that night carrying a paper sack containing her sandals. She believed that if someone prayed for her, she would not need her big therapeutic shoes. Healing is most likely to happen not only when the persons praying can let Jesus' love flow through them, but when the one receiving prayer can, like Pauline, soak up that love and expect that love to heal.

Praying with the healing love of Jesus is so simple that we can pray, as in Pauline's case, without even using words. If we are praying for another, all we have to do is let ourselves become Jesus. "To become Jesus" means that it is "no longer I who live but Jesus who lives in me" (Gal 2:20). So, for instance, when we reach out to pray, we can try to reach out with the same compassion as Jesus, even asking him where he would place his hand, and how he would place it. Then it is just a matter of letting Jesus' love flow in our own unique way from our hearts, through our hands, and into the person. As we become Jesus, we will know if there is anything we are to say or do to give his love, or if we should just silently be Jesus loving.

When we let go and become Jesus, then the Spirit will guide us as the Spirit guided Jesus to channel prayerfully the Father's healing love. This happens not when *we have the Spirit* but when we let *the Spirit have us*. To be Jesus means to want to be led by the Spirit whether he leads us to mourn or weep or sing and dance, to death or resurrection. We walk where the Spirit leads rather than lead the Spirit where we have chosen to walk. When the Spirit leads us to garden, visit the sick, or cook a meal, we will find ourselves being Jesus—open to giving and receiving love with the Father and others in the present moment, rather than only wishing the task was completed. Spiritual direction, retreats, marriage encounter, cursillo, and parish renewal programs can also sensitize us to be Jesus guided by his Spirit. The more we become Jesus in each activity we do, the more we will be Jesus as we pray with the word, infinite power, and way of the Spirit.

To become Jesus does not mean that we cease to be ourselves. In fact, we become more truly ourselves than ever before, just as we do in any deep and authentic love relationship. The more firmly we possess our self the more we can surrender to the Spirit, and the more we surrender to the Spirit the more we find our self. Thus, any activity, program or relationship that helps "our hidden self to grow strong" (Eph 3:16) and that calls us to love authentically helps us to become Jesus led by the Spirit.

But it is not just activities, programs or relationships that allow us to more and more be Jesus led by the Spirit. We can also pray with one another for a further outpouring of the Spirit as the apostles did.[1] In Acts 2, on Pentecost the Spirit came upon the people, and they prophesied, spoke in tongues and went forth boldly. But in Acts 4, the Sadducees imprisoned two of these people, Peter and John. After the Sanhedrin released them, Peter and John needed the gift of boldness again in order to be Jesus and continue to preach and heal "with cures and signs and wonders to be worked in the name of Jesus" (Acts 4:29–31). They and their friends therefore prayed for this gift, and "they were all filled with the Holy Spirit and continued to speak God's word with boldness." Whenever we find ourselves not able to be Jesus, whenever we are weak or don't know how to pray, we can pray with each other for another outpouring of the Spirit and expect that Acts 4 will happen to us too.

If we are called by the Spirit to pray with another, then we should expect that the Spirit wants to fill us with his gifts that will guide and empower our prayer. In particular we are to pray for the gifts of healing, prophecy, discernment of spirits and tongues (1 Cor 12:8; Rom 12:6–8; Eph 4:11), which help us love another in prayer as Jesus does (1 Cor 14:1–2). Since Jesus wants us all to be guided by his Spirit, we can expect that these gifts will be given to all in ordinary ways (gifts) and to a few in extraordinary ways (charisms). For example, if we have Jesus within us, we all have the gift of praying as Jesus for healing, but less healing sometimes may occur than when Francis Mac-Nutt, Barbara Shlemon or someone with a charism for healing prays. However, the more we exercise our ordinary gift for healing, the more we become Jesus loving the sick and thereby grow in praying with the depth

and power of the Spirit. Gifts grow as we pray for the Spirit's outpouring and gratefully use the Spirit's gifts to love as Jesus. For instance as I (Matt) continually pray for the Spirit's outpouring of the gifts of healing and preaching, I find that the more I use these gifts, the more they grow. Fewer fall asleep during my preaching and more are healed at a greater depth than when I first started using these gifts.

Gifts such as preaching and healing often build upon our natural abilities and skills as we ask the Spirit to let these abilities become ways of loving as Jesus. For instance, in high school I developed the skill of speaking while on the debate team. The gift of speaking has become more of a charism since others prayed with me asking the Spirit to let this speaking ability help me be Jesus. We prayed for the gift of my being able to speak as Jesus, that is, to have Jesus' love for the Father and for the people I am speaking to. The more I love as Jesus, the more the Spirit pours out this gift of preaching. Thus one way to pray for gifts is to look at our natural abilities and skills and ask that they become filled with the Spirit and become ways of loving as Jesus.

Not only speaking skills but any natural ability or interest that helps us to love can be the foundation for a charism. I (Sheila) learned this the first time I prayed for physical healing. I had a friend whose frequent migraine headaches would last for days and were not relieved by prayer or medical treatment. One day when we were working together on a project, my friend got a headache and was unable to continue working. I prayed for him and within thirty minutes his headache was gone. We were both amazed, especially when the same thing happened again a few days later. My friend said he thought that the reason my prayer had healed him was because when I prayed I seemed to love the very cells of his body for their own sake. He believed that the veins in his head "knew" this and thus relaxed. I thought back to all the times since early childhood when I had sat for hours entranced by a leaf, a stone, or a bug. I still sometimes pray by silently contemplating nature. I realized that my natural love for created things had become the foundation for a charism to pray for healing for my friend as I became Jesus in affirming the cells and calling them back to life.

The more we become Jesus, the more we will also move into other gifts such as prophecy. St. Paul urges us: "Make love your aim, and earnestly desire the spiritual gifts, especially that you may prophesy. . . . He who prophesies speaks to men for their upbuilding, their encouragement and consolation" (1 Cor 14:1–3). Prophecy is usually not a foretelling of the fu-

---

1. For the view of St. Thomas on many outpourings of the Spirit, cf. Francis Sullivan, "Baptism in the Spirit," *New Covenant*, June 1982, p. 27. This is also a chapter in his excellent book covering the Spirit's release of charisms, *Charisms and Charismatic Renewal: A Biblical and Theological Study* (Ann Arbor: Servant, 1982).

ture but simply speaking God's word (often in the first person) to the present situation. For example, as I prayed with Cindy (Chapter 6) and moved deeper into Jesus' love for her, I shared with her the words Jesus seemed to be telling her.

> You are special to me because of everything you have gone through. No other hand takes your place. Let me hold your hand like no one else ever has. . . . You belong to me, and I won't let go of you, forever. There is nothing you face that I can't walk through with you.

Cindy shared that this was the most moving part of our prayer because in my words of prophecy, she heard Jesus speak to her and felt him removing her fear.

Prophecy ranges from the ordinary gift of sharing God's words, such as the prophecy for Cindy, to the extraordinary charism of a St. Catherine of Siena (1347–1380) who could tell Pope Gregory XI that God was telling him to return from Avignon to Rome. Many in the Charismatic renewal have received an extraordinary degree of this prophetic gift while praying with another. One friend, Karen, was praying with Gary who worked on a secret government weapons project. As she focused on what Jesus wanted to say about Gary's depression, she started to see that the depression was rooted in Gary's struggle to work on an immoral project. Karen then saw in detail his laboratory and to his amazement told him everything that had been top secret—even what he did that day. She finished with prophecy, the words of Jesus asking Gary to give up his job. This so startled Gary that he began to seriously pray over whether to keep his job, and a few months later he discerned that he was to leave. His depression left too.

Through prayer Jesus has also healed many others with depression or phobias by giving a "word of knowledge" as to what trauma caused the depression or phobia. Once the trauma is located, they can return to the scene and take in Jesus' love as Linda did in her prayer healing sexual abuse (Chapter 3).

Gifts such as the word of knowledge or prophecy can be misused when we forget that to become Jesus does not mean that we cease to be ourselves. I recall a woman, Susan, who frequently gave prophecies at meetings. Her prophecies were long and repetitive. Most members of the group felt unloved as she spoke, but they were hesitant to ask her to stop for fear they would "quench the Spirit." Then one day Susan gave a prophecy to an individual, Mary, in which she predicted certain events. Mary was frightened by the prophecy and told Susan that she could not accept the prophecy as accurate. Susan became angry at Mary

and insisted that it must be accurate: "When I prophesy, it's the Spirit speaking and not me. How could the Spirit be wrong?" Susan did not know that prophecy, like other gifts, comes through us and is affected by our unique manner of speech, attitudes, and subconscious needs. Susan's prophecies were from the Spirit *and* from herself; few gifts are exercised in pure form and thus every prophecy needs to be discerned. The test of every gift is whether it leads us (or the group) to love God and others more. Since Susan's prophecies generally did not help Mary or the group to love more, it is questionable to what extent the prophecies were from the Spirit.

Besides prophecy, another gift which allows us to be Jesus is the gift of discerning spirits. Linda's healing (Chapter 3) utilized this gift. For weeks she could not forgive herself. We became aware of Linda's need for deliverance prayer, but we did not know which evil spirits were afflicting her or how they entered. So we called a friend, Joan, who has a gift of discerning spirits. Joan prayed and told us what evil spirits were present and how they entered. At the next Eucharist we prayed a deliverance prayer commanding those evil spirits to depart. Linda immediately experienced God's presence and freedom to forgive. Although not every trauma invites evil spirits of self-condemnation, incest, resentment, fear, etc., some major ones do and can be touched by deliverance prayer after everything else has been tried. Though anyone can pray deliverance prayer for themselves or *for* another, deliverance prayer *with* another should be prayed under the guidance of pastoral authorities, not by "lone rangers." The tradition, practice, and guidelines for this prayer are treated in *Deliverance Prayer*.[2]

Even though deliverance prayer with another is for the more advanced, discernment of spirits is for everyone. St. Ignatius of Loyola in his *Spiritual Exercises* wisely presents criteria for discernment of spirits and expects that retreatants will become adept at recognizing the movements of both the evil spirit and the Holy Spirit. Again this is a gift of the Spirit not just for those in the charismatic renewal but for all who pray.

The charismatic renewal is often identified with those who speak in tongues. Tongues is not just an extra gift but is mentioned fifty-seven times in the New Testament, and Paul states, "I want you all to pray in tongues" (1 Cor 14:5). Even in Augustine's fifth century church it was still the common practice to sing at Eucharist in tongues by first singing "Alleluia" and

---

2. Dennis and Matthew Linn (eds,), *Deliverance Prayer, op. cit.*

then extending the last syllable in vowel sounds of "jubilation" or wordless praise. Tongues are not a language but vocal contemplation much as when we say the rosary and pay more attention to contemplating the mysteries rather than to the words whose sounds help us stay centered in the mystery. The sounds in tongues help us stay centered on God as we love, praise, petition, thank, or adore him in a way that goes beyond words. It is a gift given because we don't know how to pray and need the Spirit to express what can't be put into words (Rom 8:26).

Tongues can be a powerful gift for praying with another, especially when we don't know how to pray. Last month we visited Sr. Erna Schmid who directs the John Bosco Vocational Training Institute in Seoul, Korea for street boys who are too emotionally disturbed to settle into a school routine. She takes time to pray with the more emotionally disturbed. Most of them are orphans who know nothing about their early traumas. After she listens to whatever problems they share, she begins to pray in tongues asking the Spirit to heal the known and the hidden hurts. Sometimes certain hurts come to mind as she prays and then she has the boy forgive those who hurt him. But other times she just prays for a certain year in a boy's life for as long as she is moved to pray in tongues. She does this for about a half hour over three days and finds that the disturbed behavior, even as consistent as nightly bed wetting, ceases and is replaced by the Spirit's gifts of joy, peace, patience, gratitude, faith, hope and love.

The Spirit wants to pour his gifts not just upon Sr. Erna, Karen, and Joan, but also upon us to do infinitely more than we can ask or imagine. So ask and imagine the Spirit giving us the gifts we need to be Jesus as we pray with another.

THE SPIRIT'S INSPIRED PRAYER FOR THE SPIRIT

I kneel before the Father from whom every family in heaven and earth takes its name; and I pray that he will bestow on you gifts in keeping with the riches of his glory. May he strengthen you inwardly through the working of his Spirit. May Christ dwell in your hearts through faith, and may love be the root and foundation of your life. Thus you will be able to grasp fully with all the holy ones, the breadth and length and height and depth of Christ's love, and experience this love which surpasses all knowledge, so that you may attain to the fullness of God himself. To him whose power now at work in us can do immeasurably more than we ask or imagine—to him be glory in the church and in Christ Jesus through all generations, world without end. Amen (Eph 3:14–21).

PART II: PRAYING WITH ANOTHER FOR HEALING SEMINAR

PREFACE TO THE SEMINAR

Today the average family moves every four years and one out of two families will move permanently apart in a shattering divorce. In this age of rootlessness there is a longing to return to roots and rooted relationships, where friends really know and love each other so much that the wounds of fractured relationships are healed. This seminar helps friends to share their growth and need for healing, and then in prayer to walk together down the road to Emmaus with another friend who can ignite and heal hearts.

Thus there are two purposes to making this seminar. The first purpose is to deepen one's prayer life by learning how to better pray alone and with another in order to meet Jesus whose unconditional love can heal all hurts. Jesus' love brings not an insulating peace but a new freedom to seek God's will at any cost. The second purpose, for those making this seminar with another, is to build a friendship deep enough to mutually share joys and hurts while learning how to better pray with each other for healing.

The seminar's first eight lessons correspond to the first eight chapters of this book. Thus sessions one through four focus on the healing power of Scripture when praying alone or with another and sessions five through eight on the process of how to pray with another. For those who wish to focus in depth on healing grief at the loss of a loved one, sessions nine through twelve focus on the healing power of praying alone or with another when grieving a death. (*Healing the Greatest Hurt*, by Dennis and Matthew Linn, S.J. and Sheila Fabricant, to be released by Paulist Press in 1985, will discuss in depth the material in sessions eight through twelve.)

We have taught this course in parishes, schools, retreat houses and hospitals, to laity, religious, married couples and those who are in the healing professions. The seminar is for anyone wishing to pray alone or with another in order to grow in giving and receiving love with Jesus or another. When friends walk with Jesus the road leads to Emmaus and the building of community.

The format of the twelve weekly sessions is as follows: welcome and prayer, a half-hour presentation in either audio or videotape form, companion sharing and companion prayer, as well as other optional experiences. The session, lasting from thirty minutes to two hours depending on how many options are included, can conclude with an open-ended snack time to deepen friendships through informal sharing. Although there are three themes of four lessons each offered here, a group may choose to take only a part of the seminar using whatever lessons they wish. Between group meetings, each participant is encouraged to pray daily for ten minutes and to journal for five minutes. Each group is encouraged to tailor the seminar to meet their needs. The emphasis is not on a rigid format but on walking with Jesus wherever he goes.

Praying with Another for Healing differs from our previous work, *Prayer Course for Healing Life's Hurts*. Whereas this book emphasizes more praying with another, *Prayer Course for Healing Life's Hurts* emphasizes more the process of praying alone. Since praying for another requires a foundation in praying alone, if you are just beginning to learn to pray, we suggest that you might wish to begin with *Prayer Course for Healing Life's Hurts*.

EXPECTATIONS:
FORMAT AND CONTENT

This seminar is divided into three themes or aspects of healing prayer:

Theme 1:
Healing Through Scripture Prayer
Theme 2:
Healing Prayer with Another
Theme 3:
Healing the Greatest Hurt

You may wish to use all three themes, or you may wish to pick out only one or two that are of special interest to you.

Similarly, you may wish to use all of the group and home experiences suggested here, or you may wish to adapt the format to meet the needs of your group and the amount of time available. Following is a description of some group and home experiences which you might choose from:

I. Group Experiences
(By ''group'' is meant two or more people.)

A. COMMON OPENING PRAYER AND SONG
(5 minutes).

At the beginning of each session, your group may wish to begin with a prayer or song to thank God for all that he has done and to ask him to help you to be receptive to his love.

B. INTRODUCTORY SHARING (10 minutes).

A time to ''get caught up'' with your companion, by sharing with each other what touched you most (in your prayer or outside of it) during the previous week.

C. VIDEO OR AUDIO TAPE (30 minutes).

A tape is presented which describes some aspect of healing and usually ends with a prayer to receive that gift of healing. In several cases, the tapes contain actual examples of persons receiving prayer for healing. Ideally, the tapes are to be used with each session. If, however, you do not have the taped teaching, you may obtain similar content for sessions one through eight from the corresponding chapter in the first section of this book.

D. SILENT REFLECTION (3 minutes).

Each person remains quiet in order to get in touch with what part of this session's tape was most moving.

E. GUIDED JOURNALING (10 minutes).

A guided experience of ''writing prayer,'' where we share with the Lord in writing what is in our heart and then listen for his response.

F. COMPANION SHARING
(5 minutes minimum for
each person to share).

Companions share with one another their response to the following questions:

1. What moved you most in today's tape and prayer? (Perhaps you will want to share what you have just written during the guided journaling.)

2. What are you most grateful for now and how do you need Jesus' help?

G. COMPANION PRAYER (5 minutes minimum
of prayer for each person).

Companions pray for each other, giving thanks for what each is most grateful for and asking for whatever way each needs Jesus' help.

H. GROUP SHARING (15 minutes).

The whole group shares what was most moving in this session's tape. Group members might also wish to share how they are growing and struggling in the seminar thus far, in order to give thanks for the growth and to support one another in the struggles.

I. CLOSING SNACK AND CELEBRATION

An open-ended time to enjoy one another and to continue sharing.

II. *Home Experiences*

A. DAILY HEALING PRAYER *(10 minutes).*

Each lesson suggests several options for daily prayer. Most of the prayers focus on the area of healing presented in that lesson. The lessons also include an "Embrace Prayer," which has no special focus but is simply a prayer of receiving love. Choose a prayer that seems helpful. Feel free to repeat all or part of that same prayer the following day and for as many days as you wish or to return to a prayer from a previous lesson. On some days, it may be more life-giving for you not to choose any of the suggested prayers but instead to be with the Lord in some other way.

B. DAILY JOURNAL *(5 minutes).*

The journal writing is done immediately after the healing prayer. Before writing, take a moment to share with Jesus where you found gratitude for growth or longing for healing during the prayer or during the day. You may wish to focus especially on the area of healing presented in that week's lesson. Then write how Jesus responds (what he says or does) to what you have just told him. If you can't get in touch with how Jesus responds, write what most moves you as you speak to him or what are the most loving words you want him to say to you. (See Appendix A, "Journaling: Writing a Love Letter," for instructions.)

C. OPTIONAL REFLECTION QUESTIONS

(for group sharing or personal reflection at home).

These questions focus on how your life experience relates to the area of healing presented in a given session.

D. OPTIONAL SUGGESTED READING.

Since each of the first eight seminar sessions corresponds to the same numbered chapter in this book (e.g., seminar Lesson 4 corresponds to Chapter 4), you may wish to read that corresponding chapter during the following week as a way of reviewing that seminar session. Our book *Healing the Greatest Hurt* (to be published by Paulist Press in 1985) may be used to accompany seminar sessions nine through twelve. Additional readings from Scripture and other sources are designed to help you explore further the questions that come to you as you reflect on each of the sessions.

As suggested above, you may wish to adapt the format presented here, according to the needs of your group and the length of your meetings. Following are possible variations for groups meeting from thirty minutes to one and a half hours or longer.

30-minute session:
Watch videotape or listen to audio tape only.

45-minute session:
Tape, Silent Reflection, Companion or Group Sharing.

60-minute session:
Tape, Silent Reflection, Companion or Group Sharing, Companion Prayer.

90-minute session
Introductory Sharing, Tape, Silent Reflection, Guided Journaling, Companion Sharing, Companion Prayer, Group Sharing.

Longer than 90 minutes:
Include the Optional Reflection Questions during the Group Sharing.

In addition to these variations in format, you may also wish to vary the timing of the seminar. The times suggested are minimal. Thus you may wish to spend more time with each part of a lesson (e.g., Companion Sharing, Companion Prayer), as well as more time for the entire lesson (perhaps meeting every two or three weeks instead of weekly). If you are using all three themes, you may wish to use one of the Optional Sessions suggested in the Appendix after each theme and before going on to the next one. Or, you may wish to skip a meeting after each theme and take a vacation in order to rest and integrate the experience of the seminar.

Perhaps you will want to take this seminar alone, using only the book or the tape and having the home experiences. But ideally this seminar should be shared with one or more companions. The best companion would be the person with whom you are most comfortable sharing, and so you may wish to invite your best friend to take this seminar with you. It is not necessary that you have prayed with this person before, as the seminar is designed to help you learn to pray together.

Besides sharing the group experiences, companions (especially married couples or others sharing the same home) may also decide to do some of the home experiences together.

Perhaps you and your companion(s) wish to take this seminar with a larger group. Ideally, larger groups should be broken into smaller groups for Companion Sharing and Companion Prayer. A group of two promotes intimacy and allows more time for each person to share, while a group of three may sacrifice some depth of sharing but increase its variety. If you don't know your companion well, you may feel more comfortable in a group of three. The final choice of a companion for Companion Sharing and Companion Prayer should ordinarily be made at the second session. Unless difficulties arise, remain with this companion throughout the whole seminar.

In considering all the options for format, timing and choice of companion, what is most important is that you meet the Lord and allow him to be with you in the most loving way. Prayer is always healing if we are simply grateful for whatever was given and even for the struggle which teaches us that without Jesus we can do nothing. Prayer is a gift and sometimes all our effort can do is to quiet us so we can open our heart as St. Teresa of Avila says, "Not to think much but to love much." These teachings and prayers merely offer possible ways to meet Jesus but each of us must follow our heart rather than the instructions. The instructions are like directions in a cookbook, mere guidelines that every good cook ignores because she likes a little less salt or more sugar. Feel free to ignore any instructions which get in the way of "loving much."

(For other considerations and options, such as what a group leader does, suggestions for journaling, Scripture prayer helps, optional sessions and where to order materials, see Appendix.)

COMMITMENT TO JESUS AND TO COMPANION(S)

Because I want to give my life entirely to the Lord Jesus Christ, I commit myself to full involvement in this seminar. This means that I will cooperate with Jesus in trying to be as faithful as possible to the following:

1. I will strive to attend each meeting.

2. During the meetings, I will share as honestly as I can with my companion(s).

3. I will prepare for each meeting by praying for a minimum of ten minutes each day and journaling for five minutes.

4. I will pray every day *for* my companion(s) and I will pray *with* my companion(s) at the meetings.

5. Out of reverence for my companion(s), I will keep anything that is shared in confidence.

6. I agree to be a companion (not a savior or advice-giving counselor), being vulnerable in sharing my own experience to the extent that I can and reverently taking to heart the sharing of another in a deep love that affirms all the good that is hidden within him or her. I cannot take away problems or pain, but I will empathically listen and pray with my group so that we can grow in commitment to the Healer. I agree to be a companion with Jesus Christ so that I might grow in the process of giving and receiving his love with those he loves.

7. If I find myself struggling with the course in a way that I am unable to work through myself, I will share my struggle with the group leader or someone else who can help me. If I do not find adequate help in the group, I will seek help—even professional help, if necessary—outside the group.

THEME 1: HEALING THROUGH SCRIPTURE PRAYER

Summary

Have you ever wished that God would speak directly to you instead of to everybody else? Or have you ever wondered if what you hear is really from God or just your own wishful thinking? Theme 1 focuses on Scripture prayer, because Scripture is one way Jesus can speak to you directly. What you hear in Scripture is his word, not just your own wishful thinking.

Lesson 1, "Healing Power of Scripture Prayer," helps you enter into Scripture prayer by inviting you to take the steps of trading hearts with Jesus: first, to get in touch with what you are feeling (grief, gratitude, sinfulness, etc.), and then, second, to enter a scene in Scripture where either Jesus or someone else is feeling the same way (e.g., Mary grieving over Jesus in John 19:25ff., Jesus' gratitude for Lazarus in John 11:42, the prostitute's sorrow for her sinfulness in Luke 7:36). Healing will happen as you enter that scene and allow Jesus (or someone else in the scene) to say and do for you the loving things Jesus wishes to say and do, until you can live out Jesus' reactions in your own situation.

Lesson 2, "Scripture Prayer with Judy for Healing Grief," exemplifies a twenty-five minute Scripture prayer that heals. As Judy remembers her mother struggling for breath and dying with a terrible thirst, she wonders how a loving God could allow such a painful death. Judy then trades hearts as she joins Mary at the foot of the cross while Jesus both struggles for breath and dies with a terrible thirst. As Judy comforts Mary struggling with Jesus' death and then allows Mary to comfort her as she struggles with her own mother's death, Judy sees her mother's death in a whole new light. Her mother's painful death no longer seems like a terrible punishment sent by God: rather, Judy knows that Jesus and Mary were "just as concerned as I was" because they had been through the same thing.

If Judy had not faced her feelings about God's seeming absence during her mother's painful death, Judy would not have been able to trade her heart with Mary and Jesus, and she probably would have blocked the healing power of her Scripture prayer. Lesson 3, "Blocks to Healing Prayer," explores unfaced feelings and other blocks to prayer. Having faced these blocks, you will in Lesson 4, "Healing Through Shared Scripture Prayer," be able to enter into that lesson's guided experience of shared Scripture prayer in a way that allows God to speak his healing word directly to you.

THEME 1: HEALING THROUGH SCRIPTURE PRAYER

Lesson 1: Healing power of scripture prayer

I. Group Meeting

A. COMMON OPENING PRAYER AND SONG
(5 minutes)

B. INTRODUCTIONS *(15 minutes)*

Take time for all present to introduce themselves and to share what they hope for from this seminar. If the group is small, all present might also share what they do or what gives them life. The group leader might begin, and then go around in a circle.

C. VIDEO OR AUDIO TAPE: *"Healing Power of Scripture Prayer" (30 minutes)*

(Ideally the taped teachings are to be used with each session. If, however, you do not have the taped teaching, you may obtain similar content from the corresponding chapter in the first section of this book. You may wish to take five minutes of silence to review the corresponding chapter and then end with either the chapter's or the session's closing prayer.)

How can Scripture prayer have the power to heal us?

1. The process of trading hearts is one we often experience, as when we are with people who are praising God and we catch their spirit of praise, or when we are with a depressed person and we too begin to feel depressed. So too we can take on the feelings and attitudes of Jesus by joining him in the events of his life (e.g., Dennis and the silver dollar, psychiatric patients, family, Matt in the Holy Land, priest and the Gerasene demoniac).

2. Sometimes we don't even know what is hurting us, but Jesus will lead us to the place in Scripture where he knows we most need his love (e.g., Sr. Ann and Jesus at Bethlehem).

3. Scripture prayer has the power to change whole social structures (e.g., Daddy King).

4. We begin to tap into the power of Scripture prayer by doing two things, as illustrated by Dennis' prayer with Judy.

- Get in touch with how we're feeling.
- See where Jesus or another was feeling the same way and then live out Jesus' reactions (e.g., Judy is frightened at seeing her dying mother struggling for breath and experiencing a terrible thirst. Judy joins Mary at the foot of the cross watching as Jesus struggles for breath and experiences terrible thirst. Judy does this until she can live out Jesus' and Mary's reaction of deep trust of the Father in the midst of physical agony and seeming abandonment).

Closing Prayer

Trading hearts with Jesus.

- Enter the scene.
  Close your eyes and imagine yourself walking down the road to Emmaus. Feel the stones underneath your feet and the hot day. Feel the perspiration trickling down your forehead. Smell the dust on the road.
- Share your heart with Jesus.
  Get in touch with whatever is in your heart that you want to share. Perhaps it's fear, or anger, or a desire to change yourself, or gratitude. Get in touch with what you are feeling and share it with Jesus for a few minutes.
- Let Jesus share his heart with you.
  When you have finished sharing you heart with Jesus, look into his eyes and take in what he is saying to you from the Scriptures. Perhaps he

will tell you how he responded to someone in Scripture who was feeling what you are feeling, or perhaps he will tell you about when he felt the same way himself. Spend a few minutes taking in what Jesus says to you until you can live out his reactions.

(The Closing Prayer for each lesson invites you to pray for some aspect of Jesus' healing love. The prayers ask you to imagine with all your senses, but visual images are stressed more than sound, touch, smell or taste. Each person is unique in the use of imagination, and some people can picture things easily while others say they "never see anything." Feel free to use your imagination in whatever way is most comfortable for you, e.g., through the senses of hearing or touch rather than through visual images.

You may find that you need a longer time for the Closing Prayer than is given on the tape. If so, the group leader might wish to lead the group through the prayer after the tape is over, allowing longer silences for each part of the prayer.)

D. SILENT REFLECTION *(3 minutes)*

Quiet time to get in touch with what moved you most in today's tape and prayer.

E. GUIDED JOURNALING *(10 minutes)*

1. Write down what is in your heart. Write as if you were writing a love letter to your best friend—Jesus—sharing what you feel most deeply. Don't worry about having the "right" words, but only try to share your heart.

2. Now get in touch with Jesus' response to you, as he is already speaking to you within. You might do this by asking what are the most loving words that you could hear in response, or perhaps by imagining that what you have just written is a note to you from the person you love most, and you want to respond to that person in the most loving possible words.

3. Write Jesus' response. Perhaps it will be just one word or one sentence. You can be sure that anything you write which helps you to know more clearly that you are loved and empowers you to love is not just your own thoughts or imagination but is really what Jesus wants to say to you.

4. One or two people in the group might want to share what they have written with the whole group.

F. COMPANION SHARING

(5 minutes minimum for each person to share)

Share your experience of the tape's closing prayer with the person next to you. (During the next session you will be asked to choose a prayer companion for the rest of the course.) You might wish to share what you wrote during the Guided Journaling.
What did you want from Jesus?
What event of Jesus' life did you find him in?
How was Jesus present to you—what did he say and do?

G. GROUP SHARING *(15 minutes)*

Share with the whole group what moved you most in today's tape and prayer.

H. CLOSING SNACK AND CELEBRATION

An open-ended time to enjoy one another and continue sharing.

II. Home experiences

A. DAILY HEALING PRAYER *(10 minutes)*

You may wish to use one of the following prayers. Feel free to repeat the same prayer for as many days as you wish, or to pray in some other way.

1. *Session's Closing Prayer*
Return to any moment in the session's closing prayer that moved you.

2. *Emmaus Prayer*
Walk with Jesus on the road to Emmaus and speak with him about your life. What event from his own life does he share with you that seems to summarize your whole life? Your past year? Your present life and the direction you are moving in? Summarize what Jesus tells you about how he is reliving in you an event in his life.

3. *Embrace Prayer*
(Before we can face our own hurts or reach out to heal another, we need to know that we are loved. If what you are most in touch with is your need to experience God's love for you, you may wish to pray this prayer for as many days as needed until you feel filled.)

See Jesus standing before you or seated in a rocking chair. See him open his arms and invite you to him. Go to him, letting him hold you and perhaps rock you in the chair. Feel his arms around you and let yourself be loved as if you were a small child in its father's arms. (You may want to pray in a similar way with the Father or with Mary as your mother. Perhaps you will better be able to experience love by seeing yourself as the one embracing, e.g., picture yourself holding a child with Jesus. Or, you might want to pray this prayer at Eucharist, letting Jesus hold you in his arms as you receive Communion.)

B. DAILY JOURNAL
(5 minutes; see Appendix A,
"Journaling: Writing a Love Letter")

Review your prayer or day and write briefly for five minutes, sharing with Jesus where you felt the most growth or where you felt the most longing for healing. Then listen as Jesus shares with you how he sees your prayer or day, and write his response. (Perhaps you and Jesus might share how he is reliving in you an event in his life.)

C. OPTIONAL REFLECTION QUESTIONS
(For group sharing or personal
reflection at home.)

1. If you could be present at an event in Jesus' life, which one would you choose?

2. Which event in Jesus' life would you fear to be present at?

D. OPTIONAL SUGGESTED READING
Each week you may wish to read the chapter in the first section of this book which corresponds to the ses-

sion you have just experienced, e.g., this week you may wish to read Chapter 1.

Scriptures (See Appendix B, "Scripture Prayer Helps")
Luke 24:13–35: Jesus revealing the Scriptures on the road to Emmaus.
Ephesians 3:14–21: Paul's prayer that we have the heart of Christ.
Luke 4:16–21: The event Jesus used to summarize his own life.
John 17:20–26: Jesus praying for us to be one with him.

Reading Scripture as the Word of God, by George Martin (Ann Arbor: Word of Life, 1975). Excellent guide to reading Scripture, both in understanding its originally intended meaning and in finding the special meaning it has for us in this moment.
Sadhana, by Anthony DeMello, S.J. Available from Institute of Jesuit Sources, 3700 W. Pine Blvd., St. Louis, Mo. 63108. This book describes forty-seven different ways of praying, including praying with Scripture.
Radical Prayer, by David Hassel, S.J. (Ramsey, N.J.: Paulist Press, 1983). See especially Chapter 3, "Prayer of Christ's Memories." Joining Jesus as he recalls the events of his life and letting him share with us how he remembers them.

THEME 1: HEALING THROUGH SCRIPTURE PRAYER

Lesson 2: Scripture prayer with Judy for healing grief

I. Group Meeting

A. COMMON OPENING PRAYER AND SONG *(5 minutes)*

B. INTRODUCTORY SHARING *(10 minutes)*

Share with your companion what touched you most (in your prayer or outside of it) during the previous week. (Perhaps you might wish to share how Jesus is reliving in you an event in his life.) What are you most grateful for and how do you need Jesus' help?

C. VIDEO OR AUDIO TAPE:

"Scripture Prayer with Judy for Healing Grief" (30 minutes)

How would you pray for someone who has lost a loved one and wonders how God could allow such a painful death? One of the ways to pray for such a hurt is by using Scripture prayer, as illustrated with Judy.

1. The first step in Scripture prayer is to get in touch with how we're feeling. Dennis begins the prayer with Judy by inviting her to share how frightened and helpless she felt as she watched her mother die. The most painful part for Judy was seeing her mother on a respirator, struggling for breath and experiencing terrible thirst.

2. The second step in Scripture prayer is to see where Jesus or someone else in Scripture felt the same way. Denny encourages Judy to join Mary at the foot of the cross, watching as Jesus struggled for breath and experienced terrible thirst. Judy enters this scene with all her senses, even repeating Jesus' words: "I thirst."

3. As Judy joins Mary at the foot of the cross, she begins to feel how Mary felt. Dennis invites Judy to listen, as Mary tells her all the things about Jesus' death that were hard for her to watch. Judy begins to feel very close to Mary, knowing that Mary suffered at the death of her Son just as Judy suffered at the death of her mother.

4. Judy knows now that Mary can understand how she feels, and so Dennis encourages Judy to begin to share with Mary all the things about her mother's death that were hard for her. Judy recalls being in her mother's hospital room and how frightened she was then. But now Judy sees Mary there with her, holding her. Judy is no longer frightened by this scene, because now there is someone with her who understands how she feels. Dennis asks Judy to continue picturing the scene of her mother's hospital room, and as she does so to breathe in Mary's love.

5. Judy sees Mary reach out to touch the baby that Judy is carrying in her womb, a baby that Judy's mother would not live to help care for. Judy no longer feels afraid of being in that hospital room.

6. Dennis asks Judy if there are any other fearful things or places associated with her mother's death that Judy would like to share with Mary. Judy asks Mary to be with her mother when she died. Judy is able to see herself join Mary in the hospital room at the moment when her mother died. Judy sees Mary bring Jesus into the room also.

7. Dennis asks Judy if there is anything she wants to say to her mother. Judy tells her mother that she loves her and wishes she didn't have to suffer. Judy sees Jesus holding his arms out to her mother. Judy sees her mother looking happy, full of light and as if she is forgetting about the pain already. Judy feels her desire to hold on to her mother, but at the same time she feels her desire for her mother to have the happiness of being with Jesus.

8. Dennis asks Judy if there is anything her mother, with Jesus and Mary, wants to say to her. Judy sees her mother smile, an assuring smile that says, "I'm

really O.K. I'm really not gone. I'm really still alive, even though my body's not alive anymore." Judy begins to cry with tears of relief as she realizes that there really is a life after death and that her mother still exists and is well. Judy sees her mother walk out the door of the hospital room with Mary and Jesus, looking back as if to say to Judy, "Don't worry."

9. Dennis asks Judy if she has any final prayer. Judy asks Jesus that her new feeling of closeness to Mary might continue and that Mary be her new mother. Dennis invites Judy to rest in Mary's arms for a few moments, and to breathe in Mary's love.

10. At the end of the prayer, Judy shares how much it helped her to have Mary with her during her mother's death—someone who really understood how Judy felt. Judy sees her mother's death in a whole new light now. Her mother's painful death no longer seems like a "weird punishment" sent by God. Now Judy knows that Jesus and Mary were going through that death with her and were "just as concerned as I was," because they had been through the same thing. Mary cared so much that she even reached out to offer love to the child in Judy's womb, something Judy hadn't even thought to ask for.

11. Two and one-half months after the prayer, Judy shares how the prayer has affected her life. Judy is able to feel all her feelings more deeply now, and she is less afraid of physical illness than she was before the prayer. Judy feels less longing to bring her mother back, because now Judy knows that her mother is "not just gone completely." Since the prayer, Judy knows Mary in a whole new way—not as someone distant and inhumanly perfect, but rather as someone who had human feelings and who can really understand Judy. Judy can now pray to Mary and find peace when she does. The effects of the prayer that are most important to Judy are knowing that Mary and Jesus are with her at painful moments, and feeling assured that life continues beyond death. Judy knows now that her mother is safe, and with God.

D. SILENT REFLECTION (3 minutes)
Quiet time to get in touch with what moved you most in today's tape.

E. GUIDED JOURNALING (10 minutes)
(See page **60**.)

F. COMPANION SHARING
(5 minutes minimum
for each person to share)

Share with your companion what moved you most in today's tape. End by sharing what you are most grateful for and how you need Jesus' help. (By the end of this session you should choose a prayer companion for the rest of the course.)

G. COMPANION PRAYER
(5 minutes minimum
of prayer for each person)

Pray for your companion for about five minutes, either silently or aloud in your own words. Give thanks for what your companion is most grateful for and pray for whatever your companion most needs. Then let your companion pray for you.

H. GROUP SHARING (15 minutes)
Share with the whole group what moved you most in today's tape.

I. CLOSING SNACK AND CELEBRATION
An open-ended time to enjoy one another and continue sharing.

II. Home Experiences

A. DAILY HEALING PRAYER (10 minutes)
You may wish to use one of the following prayers. Feel free to repeat the same prayer for as many days as you wish, to return to a prayer from the previous lesson, or to pray in some other way.

1. *Trading Hearts with Jesus at a Painful Moment*

- Recall a painful moment in your life when you felt alone, and perhaps even wondered why God would allow such a painful moment.
- Tell Jesus or Mary how you felt.
- Let Jesus or Mary share with you a moment when he or she felt the same way. Perhaps Jesus or Mary will bring someone else from Scripture to you, who went through a moment like yours and felt the same way.
- Let Jesus or Mary (or someone else from Scripture) be with you in your painful moment. See what he or she says or does for you and others in that situation.

2. *Embrace Prayer*
(See pages **60–61**.)

B. DAILY JOURNAL *(5 minutes)*

Review your prayer or day and write briefly, sharing with Jesus where you felt the most growth or where you felt the most longing for healing. Then listen as Jesus shares with you how he sees your prayer or day and write his response. (Perhaps you and Jesus might share where in your life you most need to trade hearts with him or another person in Scripture.)

C. OPTIONAL REFLECTION QUESTIONS
(For group sharing or personal reflection at home.)

1. When have you and Jesus gone through similar events in life and how did it help you to know he had gone through the same thing?

2. What event in Jesus' passion is most alive for you (e.g., Judy's mother and Jesus' words, "I thirst")?

D. OPTIONAL SUGGESTED READING
Scriptures

John 19:25–30: Jesus gives Mary to John—and to all of us—to be our mother.

Matthew 5:1–12: The Beatitudes, where Jesus tells us that our most painful moments will be turned into blessings.

Matthew 28:20: Jesus promises that he will be with us always.

Healing of Memories, by Dennis and Matthew Linn (Ramsey, N.J.: Paulist Press, 1974). Inviting Jesus into our painful memories and letting him help us to forgive ourselves and others.

Healing, by Francis MacNutt (Notre Dame: Ave Maria, 1974). Guide to the scriptural and theological foundations for healing prayer and to the four kinds of divine healing and their interrelationships.

Healing Prayer, by Barbara Shlemon (Notre Dame: Ave Maria, 1976). Brief, general introduction to healing prayer. Includes a section on guidelines for prayer room ministry.

THEME 1: HEALING THROUGH SCRIPTURE PRAYER

Lesson 3: Blocks to healing prayer

I. Group Meeting

A. COMMON OPENING PRAYER AND SONG

B. INTRODUCTORY SHARING *(10 minutes)*

Share with your companion what touched you most (in your prayer or outside of it) during the previous week. (Perhaps you might wish to share where in Jesus' life you most wanted to trade hearts with him.) What are you most grateful for and how do you need Jesus' help?

C. VIDEO OR AUDIO TAPE:

"Blocks to Healing Prayer" (30 minutes)

What is the most common block you experience in praying?

1. Spiritual directors say that the most common block in prayer is a person's failure to get in touch with feelings, especially negative feelings, and to let Jesus love them with those feelings.

2. What heals in prayer is to be able to share our negative feelings with Jesus, and let him love us with those feelings, as Linda did. There are four steps:

- Feel our feelings (e.g., when Linda let herself be angry at the evil done by the people who abused her).
- Ask Jesus, "When did you feel the same way?" and let him tell us (e.g., with Linda, Jesus said, "I felt this anger in the temple").
- Let Jesus say and do for us the things he wants to say and do (e.g., Jesus wanted to show Linda his anger on her behalf).
- The fourth step is to watch how Jesus moves through his negative feelings until we can move through our negative feelings in the same way (e.g., when Linda is ready for the fourth step,

perhaps she will be led to join Jesus as he is stripped of his garments (a form of sexual abuse), watch him forgive the people who abused him, and then in the same way begin to forgive the people who abused her).

3. Sometimes even when we have shared our negative feelings with Jesus and allowed him to love us with those feelings, our prayer is still blocked. We may be experiencing what Jesus did during the agony in the garden, when he shared his negative feelings and still had no sense that his Father was there for him. At these times of desolation, we can do the three things that Jesus did during his agony:

- Return to consolation (e.g., Jesus looks for the friends with whom he has felt loved).
- Change what can be changed (e.g., Jesus prays, "Father, if it be possible, let this pass from me").
- Accept what isn't going to change (e.g., Jesus surrenders to the Father and prays, "Not my will but thine be done"; Robin and Carol).

4. Five steps, all beginning with *P*, can help us to remove blocks to prayer:

- Take *prime time,* when we're awake and alert.
- Find a quiet *place* where we can really concentrate.
- Find a comfortable *posture* that feels reverent.
- Find a *passage* of Scripture that relates to how we feel.
- Focus on the *presence* of Jesus or the Father.

Closing Prayer

Get in touch with the time when you say to yourself, "I can't pray." (E.g., early in the morning, when you attend a "dead" liturgy, when you're filled with distractions, etc.)

- *Return to a time of consolation.* Recall a moment when you felt the Lord's love deeply. Take in a deep breath, so that all the consolation of that moment fills your whole body.
- *Ask the Lord to change what needs to be changed.* Join Jesus in the garden as he struggles to pray. Continue to take in deep breaths, letting Jesus love you even in the garden as he's struggling to pray. Tell Jesus about your struggle to pray and tell him what you wish he would change so that it would be easier for you to pray.
- *Accept what cannot be changed.* Continue to take in deep breaths and let the Lord's love fill you for even those moments that won't change, when you will still be tired or the liturgy will be "dead" or you will have too many distractions.

D. SILENT REFLECTION *(3 minutes)*
Quiet time to get in touch with what moved you most in today's tape and prayer.

E. GUIDED JOURNALING *(10 minutes)*
(See page **60**.)

F. COMPANION SHARING
*(5 minutes minimum
for each person to share)*
Share with your companion what moved you most in today's tape and prayer. End by sharing what you are most grateful for and how you need Jesus' help.

G. COMPANION PRAYER *(5 minutes minimum of prayer for each person)*
Pray for your companion for about five minutes, either silently or aloud in your own words. Give thanks for what your companion is most grateful for and ask for whatever your companion most needs. Then let your companion pray for you.

H. GROUP SHARING *(15 minutes)*
Share with the whole group what moved you most in today's tape and prayer.

I. CLOSING SNACK AND CELEBRATION
An open-ended time to enjoy one another and continue sharing.

II. Home Experiences

A. DAILY HEALING PRAYER *(10 minutes)*
You may wish to use one of the following prayers. Feel free to repeat the same prayer for as many days as you wish, to return to a prayer from a previous lesson, or to pray in some other way.

1. *Session's Closing Prayer*
Return to any moment in the session's closing prayer that moved you.

2. What is the situation you find it hardest to be loved in? Let Jesus be with you and love you in that situation.

3. When you are at your worst, what person in Scripture are you most like (e.g., Pilate, Thomas, Judas, Peter, prostitutes, Pharisees, sleeping apostles, tax collectors, Martha, rich young man, ungrateful lepers, etc.)? How does Jesus respond to that person and to you?

4. *Embrace Prayer*
(See pages **60–61**.)

B. DAILY JOURNAL *(5 minutes)*
Review your prayer or day and write briefly, sharing with Jesus where you felt the most growth or where you felt the most longing for healing. Then listen as Jesus shares with you how he sees your prayer or day, and write his response. (Perhaps you may wish to share with Jesus whatever most blocks you in your prayer, and listen to him tell you what he sees and how he wants to help you move through it.)

C. OPTIONAL REFLECTION QUESTIONS
*(For group sharing or personal
reflection at home.)*

1. When is it hardest for you to be with other people? What does this tell you about blocks in your personal prayer?

2. Who is the person you least like to talk to? What does this tell you about your blocks in praying with others?

3. If someone came to you for help and described your own problems in prayer, what would you tell them?

D. OPTIONAL SUGGESTED READINGS
Scriptures
Mark 14:32–42: Jesus' struggle to pray during the agony in the garden.

John 2:13–18: Jesus' anger when he drives out the money-changers who were defiling his Father's temple.

Matthew 6:5–15: When you pray, do not be like the hypocrites who seek public recognition rather than a deeper relationship of love with God.

Romans 8:26–27: We do not know how to pray, but the Spirit within us helps us in our weakness.

Feeling and Healing Your Emotions, by Conrad Baars (Plainfield, N.J.: Logos, 1979). How to experience and integrate our emotions in a healthy way. As a Christian psychiatrist, Dr. Baars discusses both the importance of forgiveness and yet the danger of forgiving prematurely, before we have fully recognized our anger.

When the Well Runs Dry: Prayer Beyond the Beginnings, by Thomas Green (Notre Dame: Ave Maria, 1979). How the experience of dryness in the later stages of prayer can lead us to greater receptivity to God's love and to discovering that what seems like darkness can actually be a close experience of God.

The Inner Eye of Love: Mysticism and Religion, by William Johnston (New York: Harper & Row, 1978). Mysticism as the center of religion and theology, and the inner eye of mystical experience as the eye of love itself. Describes the stages of the mystical journey, and how mysticism is related to practical action.

May I Hate God? by Pierre Wolff (New York: Paulist Press, 1979). Learning to share with God our anger at him rather than letting it separate us from him—and discovering that our anger at suffering and injustice is God's anger too.

Putting Forgiveness Into Practice, by Doris Donnelly (Allen, Tex.: Argus Communications, 1982). Forgiveness as the essential ingredient in peacemaking. Practical ways to discover our needs to forgive God, ourselves and others, and to put our discoveries into practice.

THEME 1: HEALING THROUGH SCRIPTURE PRAYER

Lesson 4: Healing through shared scripture prayer

I. Group Meeting

A. COMMON OPENING PRAYER AND SONG
(5 minutes)

B. INTRODUCTORY SHARING
(10 minutes)

Share with your companion what touched you most (in your prayer or outside of it) during the previous week. (Perhaps you might wish to share what has blocked you in your prayer and how you have begun to move through it.) What are you most grateful for and how do you need Jesus' help?

C. VIDEO OR AUDIO TAPE:

"Healing Through Shared Scripture Prayer" (30 minutes; allow an additional 15 to 75 minutes for prayer and sharing periods)

Part I

- Tape (Introduction, 7 minutes)
- Turn tape off and share with Jesus or the person next to you what you want from the prayer (5–15 minutes)
- Tape (Entering the passage of Jesus and the woman with the hemorrhage, 9 minutes)
- Turn tape off and pray silently (5–15 minutes)
- Tape (Matt sharing his reactions, 4 minutes)
- Turn tape off and share your reactions with your companion and two other people (5–15 minutes)

Part II

- Tape (Introduction to second period of prayer, 3 minutes)

- Turn tape off and pray silently (5–15 minutes)
- Tape (Matt sharing his reactions, 3 minutes)
- Turn tape off and share your reactions with your companion and two other people (5–15 minutes)
- Tape (Closing comments and instructions for final prayer with companion, 3 minutes)
- Turn tape off and pray with your companion (5 minutes or more)

The above prayer process can take from 1 to 1¾ hours. If you do not have this much time, you may wish to use only Part I.

How can we enter so deeply into the mind and heart of Jesus that we become him?

1. Introduction. Prayer is not doing something, but being someone . . . being Jesus. As we watch Jesus, we can not only start to think and feel like him, but we can even become him (e.g., Matt's grandparents).

2. How do we pray over the Scriptures?

- Find out what we really want (Matt feeling drained).
- Open the Gospels to a passage where Jesus is responding to a person like us, or where he's feeling the same way and the Father is responding to him (Mk 5:24–34: Jesus and woman with hemorrhage).
- Read the passage twice, once to understand what is being said, and the second time to enter the story by becoming Jesus or someone else in the scene.
- Share your experience of this with another person, or write it down (Matt aware of need to control).
- Enter more deeply into our experience by getting in touch again with what we want from Je-

sus, and then return to the same scene or to any other scene where we want to be with Jesus or as Jesus to be loved by the father (Matt chooses Mk 4:35–41 where apostles feel out of control and Jesus calms sea).

- Get in touch with what we are grateful for in the prayer, and say "Thank you, Lord." Matt thanks Jesus for the gift of being able to rest with him and trust the Father (child with dandelion).

D. GROUP SHARING (15 minutes)

Share what moved you most in today's tape and prayer with the whole group.

E. FOR THOSE GOING ON TO THEME 2:

With your prayer companion, get in a group of 4 to 6 people. Remember the names of the people in your group so you can pray for them during the week and meet with them at the beginning of next week's session. (See Daily Healing Prayer #1 below.)

For Those Not Going On To Theme 2: You may wish to consider meeting once more for Optional Session C or Optional Session D. (See Appendix.)

F. CLOSING SNACK AND CELEBRATION

An open-ended time to enjoy one another and continue sharing.

II. Home Experiences

A. DAILY HEALING PRAYER (10 minutes)

You may wish to use one of the following prayers. Feel free to repeat the same prayer for as many days as you wish, to return to a prayer from a previous lesson, or to pray in some other way.

1. *If you are returning for Theme 2:*
- Be with Jesus.
- Choose one of the people in your group and ask Jesus to show you how much he loves that person.
- Ask Jesus to show you what event in his life that person is living, and find a Scripture for the person.
- Write down on a slip of paper what Jesus tells you and write down the Scripture.

Do this for each person in your group and save the slips of paper to bring with you to the next meeting.

2. *If you are not returning for Theme 2:*
- Be with Jesus.

- Choose a member of your family or a person you work with. Ask Jesus to show you how much he loves that person.
- Ask Jesus to show you what event in his life that person is living, and find a Scripture for the person.
- Be with Jesus and watch what he says and does for the person.

3. *Preparation for Optional Sessions*
If you are planning to use Optional Session C or Optional Session D, consult the Preparatory Homework for that session.

4. *Session's Prayer Process*
Repeat the steps of the prayer process shown on the tape with:

your favorite event in Jesus' life
or
the event in Jesus' life that you have most lived
or
the passage used on the tape of the woman with the flow of blood (Mk 5:24–34).
See Appendix B, "Scripture Prayer Helps," for additional suggestions on praying with Scripture.

5. *Embrace Prayer*
(See pages **60–61**.)

B. DAILY JOURNAL (5 minutes)

Review your prayer or day and write briefly, sharing with Jesus where you felt the most growth or where you felt the most longing for healing. Then listen as Jesus shares with you how he sees your prayer or day, and write his response. (Perhaps you and Jesus might share where in his life you most want to meet each other.)

C. OPTIONAL REFLECTION QUESTIONS
(For group sharing or personal reflection at home.)

1. What are one or two things that help you enter into prayer (e.g., breathing, posture, music, a picture or icon, etc.)?

2. What is your favorite Scripture passage? What touches you most about that scene?

3. Who has you loved most and how have you become like that person in attitudes, feelings and behaviors (e.g., grandparent, friend, spouse, teacher, etc.)?

D. OPTIONAL SUGGESTED READING

Scriptures

Romans 12:3–8, 1 Corinthians 13: Each one of us is a unique part of the body of Christ.

Healing Power of the Bible, by Agnes Sanford (New York: Pillar, 1969). Mrs. Sanford said of this book, "My reason for this study is to give people the source from which nine-tenths of my own power is derived."

Images of Myself, by Jean Gill (Ramsey, N.J.: Paulist Press, 1982). We can all learn to meditate by reviving our ability to "think with our hearts" in imagery and symbolism. This book teaches us to meditate and to discover our own inner depths by entering the rich images and symbols of the Gospels.

The Other Side of Silence: A Guide to Christian Meditation, by Morton Kelsey (Ramsey, N.J.: Paulist Press, 1976). Study of Christian meditation which integrates the work of the great spiritual masters with the findings of modern depth psychology. See especially Chapter 16, "Putting Imagination to Work," on the power of Gospel images in meditation.

THEME 2: HEALING PRAYER WITH ANOTHER

Summary

How would you pray for healing with someone experiencing a painful memory or a deep hurt such as the loss of his or her best friend? The lessons of Theme 2 "Healing Prayer with Another," discuss and contain excerpts of healing prayers which exemplify the following four steps used in healing prayers:

1. Listening compassionately (Lesson 5: "Preparation for Healing Prayer").

2. Trading hearts with Jesus in the midst of the painful memory (Lesson 6 "Praying for Healing with Another").

3. Thanking God for what he has done (also Lesson 6).

4. Follow-up or encouraging those with whom

we pray to find other ways to receive even more love (Lesson 7: "Follow-up after Healing Prayer").

Although all four lessons contain short excerpts of healing prayers prayed with people experiencing a variety of hurts, Lesson 8, "Healing Prayer with Kim," is a longer prayer excerpt exemplifying all four steps of healing prayer. In that prayer, Sheila prays with fourteen-year-old Kim grieving over the loss of her best friend. Perhaps, especially through the prayer excerpts of these four lessons, you will discover how you would pray similarly or differently for healing, whether it be with Kim or someone else experiencing a painful memory or a deep hurt. The steps and suggestions in these lessons are merely guidelines to the goal of letting Jesus show you the unique way he prays through you.

THEME 2: HEALING PRAYER WITH ANOTHER
Lesson 5: Preparation for healing prayer

I. Group Meeting

A. COMMON OPENING PRAYER AND SONG
(5 minutes)

B. FOR THOSE WHO ARE CONTINUING FROM LESSON 4: SMALL GROUP SHARING
(15 minutes)

Join your companion and the other 2 to 4 people you met with at the end of the previous session. Share with your companion what event you see Jesus is living out in him or her now (see Daily Healing Prayer #1 for Lesson 4). After sharing with each other, hand each other the slips of paper indicating the place in Scripture you think most speaks to his or her situation. Continue to share in this way with each other person in your group.

FOR THOSE WHO ARE BEGINNING THE SEMINAR WITH THIS SESSION
(15 minutes)

Take time for all present to introduce themselves and to share what they hope for from this seminar. If the group is small, all present might also share what they do or what gives them life. The group leader might begin and then go around in a circle.

C. VIDEO OR AUDIO TAPE:
"Preparation for Healing Prayer"
(30 minutes)

How do you know where to begin when you are praying with another person?

1. Praying with another is healing to the degree he or she experiences Jesus' love through you.

2. The first step is to listen with compassion that loves the person rather than just with concern to solve the problem.

3. Once you have compassion for a person, you can begin, without probing, to look at the problem together—when it began, what has helped in the past, and especially what kind of prayer helps.

4. When you have explored how prayer has helped a person in the past and what to pray for this time, you and the person can listen to Jesus together to see if there is a specific way he wants to love the person now in prayer (e.g., Cindy and the story of Jairus' daughter).

Closing Prayer

(If you are beginning the seminar with this session, you may wish to pray with the person next to you. At the next session, you will be asked to choose a prayer companion for the rest of the course.)

The Closing Prayer for each lesson invites you to pray for some aspect of Jesus' healing love. The prayers ask you to imagine with all your senses, but visual images are stressed more than sound, touch, smell or taste. Each person is unique in the use of imagination, and some people can picture things easily while others say they "never see anything." Feel free to use your imagination in whatever way is most comfortable for you, e.g., through the senses of hearing or touch rather than through visual images.

You may find that you need a longer time for the Closing Prayer than is given on the tape. If so, the group leader might wish to lead the group through the prayer after the tape is over, allowing longer silences for each part of the prayer.)

Asking Jesus for the same desire to heal as Jesus had when he reached out to the man with the withered hand, and for the same desire that man had to receive healing.

- Look at your hand. Ask Jesus, "Who is the most difficult person that you would want me to reach out my hand and pray for?"

- Join your prayer companion. (If you are at home alone, let Jesus be your companion.)
- Listen to (or read) the story of the man with the withered hand (Mk 3:1–6). As you listen (or read), if you are on the right be especially attuned to how Jesus feels, to his desire to heal. If you are on the left, listen to the story especially from the viewpoint of the man with the withered hand and get in touch with how desirous he is to receive healing.
- If you are on the left, take your hand and let it be withered. Let it represent all the ways that it is hard for you to reach out and pray for another for healing. Place the hand in Jesus' hand (the hand of the person on the right). If you are on the right, breathe Jesus' love and healing into that hand. If you are on the left, breathe in all that healing love. Let it flow into your whole body and into all the withered parts of your spirit that make it hard for you to reach out and pray with another person.
- Reverse positions, so that if you are on the left you become Jesus and if you are on the right you become the man with the withered hand.
- Take a moment of silence and see yourself now praying with that person who is difficult for you to pray for. See Jesus next to you and say the prayer that is in Jesus' heart for that person.

D. SILENT REFLECTION (3 minutes)

Quiet time to get in touch with what moved you most in today's tape.

E. GUIDED JOURNALING (10 minutes)

1. Write down what is in your heart. Write as if you were writing a love letter to your best friend—Jesus—sharing what you feel most deeply. Don't worry about having the ''right'' words, but only try to share your heart.

2. Now get in touch with Jesus' response to you, as he is already speaking to you within. You might do this by asking what are the most loving words that you could hear in response, or perhaps by imagining that what you have just written is a note to you from the person you love most, and you want to respond to that person in the most loving possible words.

3. Write Jesus' response. Perhaps it will be just one word or one sentence. You can be sure that anything you write which helps you to know more clearly that you are loved is not just your own thoughts or imagination but is really what Jesus wants to say to you.

4. One or two people in the group might want to share what they have written with the whole group.

F. COMPANION SHARING (5 minutes minimum for each person to share)

Share with your companion your experience of the tape and especially of the withered hand prayer. What touched you most? You may wish to use your last few minutes to share with each other what you most want from Jesus and to pray with each other for it.

G. GROUP SHARING (15 minutes)

Share with the whole group what moved you most in today's tape and prayer.

H. CLOSING SNACK AND CELEBRATION

An open-ended time to enjoy one another and continue sharing.

II. Home Experiences

A. DAILY HEALING PRAYER (10 minutes)

You may wish to use one of the following prayers. Feel free to repeat the same prayer for as many days as you wish, to return to a prayer from a previous lesson, or to pray in some other way.

1. *Session's Closing Prayer*
Return to any moment in the session's closing prayer that moved you.

2. Read Luke 10:38–42 about Mary listening at the feet of Jesus. Ask Jesus what one person he wants you to listen to today. Ask him how he loves that person and how he wants you to listen to that person. (During one day, let Jesus show you how he wants you to listen to your prayer companion.)

3. Read Luke 10:38–42 about Mary listening at the feet of Jesus. Thank Jesus for the people in the past day that you have listened to attentively, and ask for help with those you have struggled to listen to.

4. *Embrace Prayer*
(Before we can face our own hurts or reach out to heal another, we need to know that we are loved. If what you are most in touch with is your need to experience God's love for you, you may wish to pray this prayer for as many days as needed until you feel filled.)

See Jesus standing before you or seated in a rocking chair. See him open his arms and invite you to him.

Go to him, letting him hold you and let yourself be loved as if you were a small child in its father's arms. (You may want to pray in a similar way with the Father or with Mary as your mother. Perhaps you will better be able to experience love by seeing yourself as the one embracing, e.g., picture yourself holding a child with Jesus. Or you might want to pray this prayer at Eucharist, letting Jesus hold you in his arms as you receive Communion.)

B. DAILY JOURNAL *(5 minutes;*
see Appendix A, "Journaling:
Writing a Love Letter")

Review your prayer or day and write briefly, sharing with Jesus where you felt the most growth or where you felt the most longing for healing. Then listen as Jesus shares with you how he sees your prayer or day, and write his response. (Perhaps you may wish to share with Jesus how you are grateful for growth or long for healing in listening with a compassionate heart, and see what he says or does about it.)

C. OPTIONAL REFLECTION QUESTIONS
(For group sharing or
personal reflection at home.)

1. Who is the best listener you know? What is it about the way he or she listens that you especially appreciate?

2. Whom do you find it easiest to listen to? What makes it easy for you to listen to that person?

3. How do you know whether you are hearing the Lord or hearing your own fears and needs?

4. Read Acts 21:10–14. A prophecy or word from the Lord needs to be discerned by those who hear it. Paul comes to a different conclusion than the others who hear the Lord speaking through Agabus. Have you ever experienced that?

D. OPTIONAL SUGGESTED READING
Each week you may wish to read the chapter in the first section of this book which corresponds to the session you have just experienced, e.g., this week you may wish to read Chapter 5.

Scriptures
Luke 10:38–42. Jesus praises Martha's sister, Mary, for her ability to listen.

John 4:4–42: Jesus listens compassionately to the Samaritan woman.

Acts 21:10–14: Paul listens to the discernment of the prophet Agabus, but Paul hears the Lord saying something different to him.

Mark 3:1–7: Jesus is so eager to heal that he prays for the man with the withered hand on the Sabbath.

Luke 8:41–56: Jesus prays for Jairus' daughter.

Born Only Once: The Miracle of Affirmation, by Conrad Baars (Chicago: Franciscan Herald Press, 1975). The healing power of unconditional, affirming love. Only by receiving such love from others can we be born as our true selves.

Listening, by Morton Kelsey (leaflet published by Dove Publications, Pecos, N.M.). Brief and very beautiful description of what it means to truly listen to another person.

The Art of Christian Love, by Morton Kelsey (Pecos, N.M.: Dove Publications, 1974). Love is central to Christian life because we cannot love others unless we have first been loved. Includes a section on listening as essential to loving because we cannot know another's needs until we have heard that person share his or her world.

The Art of Christian Listening, by Tom Hart (New York: Paulist Press, 1980). How to listen to another person's story, in the informal context of family and friendship, or in the more formal settings of prayer ministry, spiritual direction, etc.

The Secret of Staying in Love, by John Powell (Niles, Il.: Argus Communications, 1974). Relationships remain vital and loving when we share what is really going on inside of us and when our sharing is received by the other with love and acceptance.

Prayer Course for Healing Life's Hurts, by Matthew and Dennis Linn and Sheila Fabricant (New York: Paulist Press, 1983). Chapter 23, "Finding God's Will." How to listen to God for guidance when we have a decision to make. The moment when we feel most loved is the moment when we can best hear God's will.

The Healing Gifts of the Spirit, by Agnes Sanford (New York: J.B. Lippincott, 1966). Guide to the healing of memories, inspired by the author's own experience of being healed of mental depression. Discusses how to know what to pray for and the sensitive process of listening to the hurting person. See especially Chapter 6, "The Gift of Knowledge," on how to use this gift wisely.

THEME 2: HEALING PRAYER WITH ANOTHER

Lesson 6: Praying for healing with another

I. Group Meeting

A. COMMON OPENING PRAYER AND SONG (5 minutes)

B. INTRODUCTORY SHARING (10 minutes)

Share with your companion what touched you most (in your prayer or outside of it) during the previous week. (Perhaps you might wish to share how you are grateful for growth or long for healing in listening with a compassionate heart.) What are you most grateful for and how do you need Jesus' help?

C. VIDEO OR AUDIO TAPE:

"Praying for Healing with Another" (30 minutes)

How do you pray with another person who has a painful memory?

1. There are four steps in praying with a person.
- Listening compassionately to the person and listening to Jesus for how he wants to be present to that person. This step was covered in Lesson 5, "Preparation for Healing Prayer."
- Help the person to trade hearts with Jesus.
- Give thanks for all that has happened.
- Follow up with the person, encouraging him or her in ways that can deepen the healing.

This session covers the second and third steps.

2. Trading hearts with Jesus begins by helping the person to focus with his or her imagination on seeing, hearing or touching Jesus, so his love is experienced more strongly than the problem. Some people cannot imagine moving closer to Jesus but can experience Jesus in a Scripture scene taking the initiative to move closer to them.

3. Once they are in touch with Jesus' love, ask what they are experiencing and keep reinforcing the ways Jesus is healing or keep drawing their attention back to Jesus if they are drifting away from prayer or into overwhelming pain. Getting in touch with too much pain at once can lead to despair; avoiding the pain that is really there can lead to little hunger for a savior and therefore to little healing. Healing is happening when the person can experience God's love in the midst of the painful memory.

4. When the person is constantly focused on Jesus and able to take in more and more of his love, and when no more pain is surfacing, then it is time to bring the prayer to a close and thank God for all that has happened.

Closing Prayer

Asking Jesus to fill us with life as he did Jairus' daughter.

- Take the hand of your companion and close your eyes. (If you are alone, let Jesus be your companion.)
- Imagine yourself as Jairus' daughter and get in touch with all the ways you want to hold Jesus' hand and all the ways you need to pull in life from him (e.g., his strength, love from the Father, risen sexuality, etc.).
- Feel the hunger in Jesus' heart to fill you, and hear him say, "Fear is useless. Even in death, what is needed is trust to bring new life." When you get in touch with how much love and power are in the heart of Jesus, begin to breathe that love and power into your body.
- Breathe out whatever is not of Jesus (e.g., fear, resentment).

- Continue to feel Jesus' life pour into you with every breath, until you can take in no more and are completely filled with Jesus to the point that even when you breathe out you are giving his life.
- When you feel the power in yourself to move in a whole new way, as did Jairus' daughter, hear the words of Jesus: ''Rise.'' Feel Jesus' strength moving your body and slowly stand up, filled with the power of Jesus.

D. SILENT REFLECTION *(3 minutes)*

Quiet time to get in touch with what moved you most in today's tape.

E. GUIDED JOURNALING *(10 minutes)*

(See page **73**.)

F. COMPANION SHARING *(5 minutes minimum for each person to share)*

Share with your companion what moved you most in today's tape and prayer. End by sharing what you are most grateful for and how you need Jesus' help.

G. COMPANION PRAYER

(5 minutes minimum of prayer for each person)

Pray for your companion for about 5 minutes, either silently or aloud in your own words. Give thanks for what your companion is most grateful for and ask for whatever your companion most needs. Then let your companion pray for you.

H. GROUP SHARING *(15 minutes)*

Share with the group your experience of the tape, especially what touched you most in your own or Cindy's prayer experience.

I. CLOSING SNACK AND CELEBRATION

An open-ended time to enjoy one another and continue sharing.

II. *Home Experiences*

A. DAILY HEALING PRAYER *(10 minutes)*

You may wish to use one of the following prayers. Feel free to repeat the same prayer for as many days as you wish, to return to a prayer from a previous lesson, or to pray in some other way.

1. *Session's Closing Prayer*
Return to any moment in the session's closing prayer that moved you.

2. Get in touch with what you want. Ask another person to pray with you. You may wish to use some of the steps used with Cindy:

- Listen.
- Center on Jesus and trade hearts.
- Give thanks.
- (Follow-up.)

3. Pray with another person. You may wish to use some of the steps used with Cindy. (You and your companion may wish to go together to pray with another person.)

4. Try and become another person by sitting as they would. Ask Jesus to help you experience everything in that person that hungers for Jesus (e.g., fears, loneliness, resentment). Let your hand become that person's hand. Take Jesus' hand and draw in his strength for that person. (You may wish to pray this prayer once during the week for your prayer partner.)

5. *Embrace Prayer*
(See page **73–74**.)

B. DAILY JOURNAL *(5 minutes)*

Review your prayer or day and write briefly, sharing with Jesus where you felt the most growth or where you felt the most longing for healing. Then listen as Jesus shares with you how he sees your prayer or day, and write his response. (Perhaps you may wish to share with Jesus what helps or hinders you in praying with another, and see what he says or does about it.)

C. OPTIONAL REFLECTION QUESTIONS
*(For group sharing or
personal reflection at home.)*

1. When have you had an experience like Cindy which changed the way you or another saw things?
2. What prayer with another moved you the most? Why? What did you learn from it?
3. What prayer with another disappointed you the most? Why? What did you learn from it?

D. OPTIONAL SUGGESTED READING
Scriptures (See Appendix B, ''Scripture Prayer Helps'')
Luke 24:13–35: The apostles trade hearts with Jesus on the road to Emmaus.

Mark 5:35–43: Jesus prays for Jairus' daughter and brings her back from the edge of death.

Mark 16:15–20: Jesus commissions his disciples to reach out and heal the sick in his name.

Ephesians 3:14–21: Paul's prayer for the Ephesians to be filled with the love of Christ.

Romans 8:35–39: Nothing can separate us from the love of Christ, not even death itself.

2 Corinthians 5:16–21: Anyone who is in Christ is a new creation.

The Prayer That Heals: Praying for Healing In the Family, by Francis MacNutt (Notre Dame: Ave Maria, 1981). A simple book about healing prayer, especially with those who are closest to us—the members of our own family.

Inner Healing: God's Great Assurance, by Theodore Dobson (New York: Paulist Press, 1978). Scriptural and theological foundations for the healing ministry, the process of inner healing and the role of forgiveness in healing. Presents inner healing as part of lifelong growth in friendship with Jesus.

The Broken Image, by Leanne Payne (Westchester, Il.: Cornerstone Books, 1981). Excellent book on inner healing prayer for homosexuality based upon the author's theological and psychological study as well as upon her experience in praying for healing.

Healing the Hidden Self, by Barbara Shlemon (Notre Dame: Ave Maria, 1982). Praying for healing of the hurts that may occur at different stages of life. Especially helpful in how to pray for hurts occurring at conception, in the womb, at birth and in infancy.

Inner Healing, by Michael Scanlan (New York: Paulist Press, 1974). General introduction to inner healing prayer—what it is, the role and authority of the person ministering healing, how to pray, and the importance of a healing community.

The Gift of Inner Healing, by Ruth Stapleton (Waco, Tex.: Word Books, 1976). Introduction to inner healing prayer using case histories to illustrate the kinds of things that can happen when we pray for another. Especially helpful in describing the use of "creative imagination."

The Experience of Inner Healing, by Ruth Stapleton (Waco, Tex.: Word Books, 1977). Suggests many ways of inner healing, e.g., through love, faith, surrender, forgiveness, confession, service to others, authentic self-identity.

THEME 2: HEALING PRAYER WITH ANOTHER
Lesson 7: Follow-up after healing prayer

I. Group Meeting

A. COMMON OPENING PRAYER AND SONG
(5 minutes)

B. INTRODUCTORY SHARING *(10 minutes)*
Share with your companion what touched you most (in your prayer or outside of it) during the previous week. (Perhaps you might wish to share what helps or hinders you in praying with another.) What are you most grateful for and how do you need Jesus' help?

C. VIDEO OR AUDIO TAPE:
"Follow-Up After Healing Prayer"
(30 minutes)

What do you do afterward to deepen a powerful experience of healing?

1. After listening with compassion, trading hearts with Jesus, and giving thanks for his healing, the fourth step of healing prayer is to follow up in ways that gratefully celebrate God's healing and open us to receive more love into our bodies, minds and spirits (e.g., Agnes Sanford and gardening).

2. An easy follow-up prayer is to pray silently with another and simply to give and receive Jesus' love through laying on of hands (e.g., Paul and Linda).

3. Not only those receiving prayer but also those praying for others must follow up with actions that help them receive love, live a balanced life and thereby avoid burn-out. Jesus is the Savior, not we.

4. We know we have recovered from burn-out when praying with others gives life to us and to those we pray with, rather than draining life from any of us.

Closing Prayer
Prayer of healing the future, using the prayer of silent touch.

- Join your prayer companion.
- As you look ahead, what do you expect to be a difficult moment this week or year?
- Get in touch with how much Jesus loves you. It may help you to recall a specific moment when you felt his love, as Paul did when he recalled his experience with his cross.
- If you are on the right, be Jesus and reach out as Linda reached out to Paul, giving Jesus' love. If you are on the left, receive that love into your difficult moment. Pray in silence, using only touch and the prayer in your heart to give and receive Jesus' love.
- After five minutes, reverse roles and pray for another five minutes.

D. SILENT REFLECTION *(3 minutes)*
Quiet time to get in touch with what moved you most in today's tape and prayer.

E. GUIDED JOURNALING *(10 minutes)*
(See page **73**.)

F. COMPANION SHARING *(5 minutes minimum for each person to share)*
Share with your companion what moved you most in today's tape and prayer. End by sharing what you are most grateful for and how you need Jesus' help.

G. COMPANION PRAYER *(5 minutes minimum of prayer for each person)*
Pray for your companion for about 5 minutes, either silently or aloud in your own words. Give thanks for what your companion is most grateful for and ask for whatever your companion most needs. Then let your companion pray for you.

H. GROUP SHARING *(15 minutes)*
Share what moved you most in today's tape and prayer with the whole group.

I. CLOSING SNACK AND CELEBRATION

An open-ended time to enjoy one another and continue sharing.

II. *Home Experiences*

A. DAILY HEALING PRAYER *(10 minutes)*

You may wish to use one of the following prayers. Feel free to repeat the same prayer for as many days as you wish, to return to a prayer from a previous lesson, or to pray in some other way.

1. *Session's Closing Prayer: Prayer of Healing the Future*
- As you look ahead, what do you expect to be a difficult moment this week or year?
- Get in touch with how much Jesus loves you. It may help you to recall a specific moment when you felt his love, as Paul did when he recalled his experience with his cross.
- With each breath, breathe Jesus' love into your difficult moment and breathe out your fears.

2. *Release Prayer*
- Place your hand on your heart.
- Ask Jesus to show you a person in your heart whom you are overly concerned about.
- Reach into your heart and take the person out.
- As you hold the person in your hand, tell Jesus how you want him to be everything you cannot be for that person.
- When you've told Jesus everything, lift up your hand to Jesus. Watch how Jesus lovingly receives the person from you and places the person in his heart. Join Jesus in loving him or her.

3. *Embrace Prayer*
(See page **73–74**.)

B. DAILY JOURNAL *(5 minutes)*

Review your prayer or day and write briefly, sharing with Jesus where you felt the most growth or where you felt the most longing for healing. Then listen as Jesus shares with you how he sees your prayer or day, and write his response. (Perhaps you may wish to share with Jesus what helps or hinders you in living a balanced life, and see what he says or does about it.)

C. OPTIONAL REFLECTION QUESTIONS

(For group sharing or personal reflection at home.)

1. What is the moment in your life when God touched you the most?

2. Just as Paul was able to move through his struggle with reading aloud in front of a group by recalling Jesus' struggle on the cross, when have you been able to get through a struggle by joining Jesus in an event of his life?

3. How is Jesus asking you to lead a more balanced life?

4. Is there one person or situation draining life from you that Jesus is asking you to say "no" to? What makes it difficult for you to say "no"?

5. Is there one person or situation that would give you life and that Jesus is asking you to say "yes" to? What makes it difficult to say "yes"?

D. OPTIONAL SUGGESTED READINGS

Scriptures (see Appendix B, "Scripture Prayer Helps")

Luke 15:11–31: The prodigal's father gives a party to celebrate and give thanks for his son's return.

John 2:1–12: Jesus takes time to enjoy himself by attending the wedding feast at Cana . . . and even provides the wine.

Luke 7:31–36: Jesus is criticized by the Pharisees for celebrating too much.

Matthew 14:22–24: Jesus takes time to go off by himself and pray.

Ministry Burnout, by John Sanford (Ramsey, N.J.: Paulist Press, 1982). How people involved in ministry become vulnerable to burnout and ways to avoid this state of spiritual exhaustion and rediscover the joy of creative service.

The Power To Heal, by Francis MacNutt (Notre Dame: Ave Maria, 1977). Chapter 9, "Having To Say No." The necessity—and difficulty—of saying "no" to people in need when we have reached our own limit.

"Ministering to Yourself," by Jeanne Hill (Pecos, N.M.: Dove Publications, Leaflet #54). How to minister to the needs we discover in ourselves as we pray for others, and how to deepen the healing we receive when others pray for us.

Healing the Unaffirmed: Recognizing Deprivation Neurosis, by Conrad Baars and Anna Terruwe (New York: Alba House, 1976). How to recognize and minister to those who did not receive affirming love in childhood and therefore suffer what the authors call "deprivation neurosis."

IS IT GETTING HARD TO PRAY OR JOURNAL?

Follow-up and give-up often go together. When follow-up touches areas of unhealed resistances (fears, anger, guilt, etc.), they shout "Give up." So, frequently by this time in the course the follow-up of prayer and journaling is effectively touching unhealed areas which resist by making it harder to pray or journal.

When I taught this course for the first time, I found that during the first sessions some people acted as if they were in love with the course and on a honeymoon. Not only would they come early to the meetings and stay late, but they were also putting in extra time at home for prayer and journaling. After about the fourth session, however, I found that some of these same people were experiencing great resistance to doing what before had given them so much life. So, I began asking people to identify their difficulty with the seminar. Their comments were focused mainly on struggles with prayer and journaling.

Some identified their struggle with prayer by saying, "I have trouble trying to do it every day, and I feel guilty when I don't." But others who were able to pray every day would say, "I feel I have to do all the prayers and there's just too much for me to do." And finally some who had time to try all the different prayers would describe their struggle by saying, "When I try to pray, nothing happens."

Besides their struggle with prayer, they also struggled with journaling. One woman showed me the blank pages of her journal and said, "I can't write. I don't have words like other people. I'm afraid I'll do it all wrong." But even some who had full pages in their journal were having difficulty. One man said, "I can't tell if it's Jesus speaking or if it's just me. It's hard for me to believe that Jesus would take time to talk with me." Another who did feel able to identify the voice of Jesus explained her struggle by saying, "I'm afraid of what

Jesus wants to say to me. I'm afraid that he will ask too much of me."

I could see that it was the goodness of these people that brought on the struggle. They loved God and were struggling only because they wanted to love him more. Their temptation was to feel that they had to do everything and to do it perfectly in order to earn God's love. They felt that something was wrong with them, that they were spiritual failures because they were having difficulties with the course. They would feel guilty and be hesitant to share what was really going on—or even be tempted to give up completely.

Breakthroughs happened when people began to identify their present struggle and then invite Jesus into the present struggle or into the past memory that seemed to be at the root of their present struggle. The story of Ann exemplifies both ways of praying.

Ann's honeymoon with the course was cut short during the first session when she learned that she would be expected to write in a journal. She was immediately aware of her lifelong difficulty in expressing herself and afraid that she could not do what would be asked of her. As the group was led through a guided journaling exercise, she wrote, "Why have I no words?" As she listened for Jesus' response, she heard him say to her, "That's why you're here." Because she experienced this response as not only Jesus' loving acceptance of her in her present struggle but also as a personal invitation to let him give her the words, she felt a desire to write down faltering words and phrases about other situations. Slowly the first page of her journal began to take shape.

Gradually Ann was able to share herself with the Lord at deeper and deeper levels through the pages of her journal. As her self-awareness developed, she came to understand that the fear of journaling she experienced during the first session of the course was part of a difficulty with self-expression which began when she was two years old and her nine-month-old brother died. Ann's mother was so traumatized by the death that she attempted suicide and Ann was sent off to stay with a grandmother. Ann was never allowed to express her feelings of fear, anger, and grief over the loss of her baby brother. She had felt ever since that all her words were bottled up inside her. Ann's deeper breakthrough came when she used Scripture prayer to identify with Jesus at the death of the Holy Innocents. Knowing that Jesus had experienced a similar hurt when he was two years old meant for Ann that now she had someone to share her bottled-up feelings. As she joined Jesus and his mother in their fear, grief and anger, Ann's own buried emotions were released and healed. Her husband, a Freudian psychoanalyst, said that years of therapy would have been required to bring about the change he saw in his wife.

Not only Ann, but many others in the seminar experienced new freedom as they invited Jesus into root memories which seemed to underlie their present struggle with prayer and journaling.

> Mary was afraid to write and felt unable to journal. She made a breakthrough when she was able to forgive a teacher who had publicly ridiculed her in the classroom for spelling "Spirit" as "sprite."
>
> Susan was struggling with prayer and journaling because she feared that if she listened to Jesus, he would ask too much of her. Susan's father was a demanding doctor who had always expected her to achieve more than she could. She was gradually able to relax and listen to Jesus after several weeks of praying the Embrace Prayer. As she repeated this prayer, the tense body of her over-achieving inner child became more and more relaxed in the Father's arms until she could be content with just resting and not trying to achieve or do anything.

Like Susan, Joan constantly crossed out what she journaled because it didn't sound like Jesus—it had mistakes and sounded too much like what she would say. Jesus took her back to her mother's funeral where her father made her promise that she would do her best to make her deceased mother proud of her forever. But this time Jesus told her, "You don't have to promise to be perfect anymore. I allow you to write mistakes so you can experience my love for you just the way you are. Knowing I love you with your mistakes is more important than writing perfectly or having the deepest insights. I even use your words because they are all beautiful to me and you understand your own words better." This led Joan to ask Jesus, "If you use my words, how do I know it's *you* speaking and not *me?*" Jesus responded, "But can't you see? We are one! I want us to always be one as the Father and I are one."

Joan wrote a twenty-page letter stating how much healing happened through her prayer and journaling. Joan ended by stating why she continues to journal daily even after the seminar.

> Just by opening up myself to Jesus' response to my letters, I always come away uplifted and hopeful. Merely writing to him doesn't quite work the same. I still may have the same feeling I started with. But after giving Jesus a chance to tell me how he sees the situation, through his eyes, I come away different—with a new vision—his vision. Every day that I write to Jesus, I can't get over the healings that come back by just taking the time to listen to him love me back.

When shared with Jesus, the time of giving-up on praying or journaling is transformed into the time of deepest healing.

THEME 2: HEALING PRAYER WITH ANOTHER

Lesson 8: Healing prayer with Kim

I. Group Meeting

A. COMMON OPENING
PRAYER AND SONG *(5 minutes)*

B. INTRODUCTORY SHARING *(10 minutes)*

Share with your companion what touched you most (in your prayer or outside of it) during the previous week. (Perhaps you might wish to share what helps or hinders you in living a balanced life.) What are you most grateful for and how do you need Jesus' help?

C. VIDEO OR AUDIO TAPE:
"Healing Prayer with Kim"
(30 minutes)

How would you pray with someone who has lost his or her best friend? The prayer with Kim puts together all the steps of praying for healing.

1. Fourteen-year-old Kim's grandmother died two years ago. Kim felt grief, anger at others for how they treated her grandmother, and guilt that she could not save her grandmother.

2. Sheila begins the prayer with Kim by listening compassionately as Kim shares her feelings. Sheila tries to enter Kim's world and let Kim know that someone understands.

3. Sheila encourages Kim to first share her memories of joyful moments with her grandmother, recalling the ways she felt loved by her grandmother.

4. Once Kim is in touch with her positive memories of being loved, Sheila leads Kim to get in touch with her hunger for Jesus' healing by asking Kim to become aware of the ways she misses her grandmother. Kim shares her loneliness for a friend like her grandmother was. Kim experiences her loneliness and grief as "this big empty place that can never be filled up," a place in Kim's heart.

5. Sheila begins the process of trading hearts by asking Kim to pretend that she (Sheila) is her grandmother, and to tell her grandmother all the ways she misses her. Then Sheila asks Jesus to help Kim hear what her grandmother wants to say in response. In this conversation between Kim and her grandmother, Kim is able to share what is in her heart by expressing her loneliness, grief, guilt, disappointment and anger that her grandmother left her.

6. Kim sees her grandmother with Jesus, looking "real healthy." Jesus shares his heart with Kim as he gives her his vision of her relationship with her grandmother. Jesus tells Kim, "It's going to be O.K. She'll always be with you, maybe not physically, but mentally and in your heart. And so will I." Jesus invites Kim to hold her grandmother's hand, and then Kim experiences being embraced by her grandmother and reunited with her.

7. Sheila tells Kim to remain with this inner experience for a while, taking in all the love that Jesus wants to give Kim through her grandmother.

8. After a few minutes, Kim is ready to move on. She says that now she feels "more confident. Like that she's O.K. and she's got the Lord and she really doesn't need me anymore. But in a way she still needs me and I still need her. But I feel now like I don't *have* to have her." Sheila says, "You both have Jesus too," and Kim answers, "Yes."

9. Sheila invites Kim to experience her new relationship with her grandmother of being united in Jesus by asking Kim to express the prayer that's in her heart for her grandmother, and then to listen for how her grandmother is praying for her. Sheila prays for this new relationship, asking that the love between Kim and her grandmother continue to grow as they send love to each other through Jesus.

10. Kim thanks Jesus for filling up the empty place in her heart with love and "a lot of circulation."

11. Sheila suggests some ways of follow-up to Kim, as in her closing prayer she encourages Kim to keep being aware of her grandmother's love for her, and of Jesus' love for her that can fill up any emptiness.

12. At the close of the prayer, Kim shares that she knows now that Jesus was not trying to send her pain and sorrow by taking her grandmother away, but rather that he wants to fill her with love and joy.

13. Two months later, Kim told us that after her grandmother died, she was afraid to ever love anyone again because she might lose that person too. But now that she knows her grandmother is still with her, she is no longer afraid to reach out to others and risk entering into new friendships. Kim added that the painful empty place in her chest has not returned, and she still feels filled with life and "circulation."

D. SILENT REFLECTION (3 minutes)
Quiet time to get in touch with what moved you most in today's tape.

E. GUIDED JOURNALING (10 minutes)
(See page 73.)

F. COMPANION SHARING
(5 minutes minimum
for each person to share)
Share with your companion what moved you most in today's tape. End by sharing what you are most grateful for and how you need Jesus' help.

G. COMPANION PRAYER
(5 minutes minimum
of prayer for each person)
Pray for your companion for about 5 minutes, either silently or aloud in your own words. Give thanks for what your companion is most grateful for and ask for whatever your companion most needs. Then let your companion pray for you.

H. GROUP SHARING (15 minutes)
Share with the whole group what moved you most in Kim's prayer.

For those going on to Theme 3: Choose which of the optional sessions in Appendix D you wish to do next week. The optional sessions we suggest are: A. Simple Ways To Pray, or B. In-Depth Prayer for Another.

If you are not going on to Theme 3: You might wish to meet again for optional session C. Gratitude for Growth Through the Seminar, or D. Gratitude for Growth Through Another.

Below is a short description of each option:

Optional Session A:
Simple Ways To Pray
The purpose of this session is to learn ways of praying that are simple (take less than 5 minutes) and to introduce you to the *Prayer Course for Healing Life's Hurts*. The session includes a 30-minute movie or video-tape showing segments of prayers (e.g., breathing prayer, writing prayer, etc.) done with eight different people. This program may be followed with a short exercise from Lesson 1, "Simple Ways To Pray," taken from the *Prayer Course* guidebook. If you have not taken the *Prayer Course*, you may wish to have this experience of the first lesson of the course and then consider the course as a possible follow-up to this seminar. (See Appendix.)

Optional Session B:
In-Depth Prayer for Another
The purpose of this session is to pray with one person for an extended period of time and then reflect on your experience of the prayer. The session begins by forming groups of four (including your prayer companion), and then choosing one member of the group to receive prayer. After 30–40 minutes of prayer for that person, all four members of the group take time to reflect together on the prayer experience. Finally, an opportunity is provided to share some of these reflections with the larger group. (See Appendix.)

Optional Session C:
Gratitude for Growth Through the Seminar
The purpose of this session is to appreciate how God has touched you and others through this seminar. Each person who wishes to might share with the whole group: What in this seminar has touched me most and changed my life? For what moment or event in this seminar do I most give thanks and why? (See Appendix.)

Optional Session D:
Gratitude for Growth Through Another
(Recommended for groups of 20 or less.) The purpose of this session is to give thanks for how each person in the group has gifted you. Take a few minutes to focus on each person and let the rest of the group members share how that person has given them life. Then let that person share how he or she has received life from the other members of the group. (See Appendix.) NOTE: You may wish to do one or more of the above optional

sessions. Consult each lesson's "Preparatory Homework" for suggestions on how best to prepare for that lesson.

I. CLOSING SNACK AND CELEBRATION

An open-ended time to enjoy one another and continue sharing.

II. *Home Experiences*

A. DAILY HEALING PRAYER *(10 minutes)*

You may wish to use one of the following prayers. Feel free to repeat the same prayer for as many days as you wish, to return to a prayer from a previous lesson, or to pray in some other way.

1. *If you are returning next week:*

Consult the Preparatory Homework for whichever optional session your group has chosen. If you are going on to Theme 3, Lesson 9 next week rather than doing an optional session, you may wish to do the Preparatory Homework for Optional Session C: Gratitude for Growth Through the Seminar.

2. *Embrace Prayer*
(See page **73–74**.)

B. DAILY JOURNAL *(5 minutes)*

Review your prayer or day and write briefly, sharing with Jesus where you felt the most growth or where you felt the most longing for healing. Then listen as Jesus shares with you how he sees your prayer or day and write his response. (Perhaps you may wish to share with Jesus what you are most grateful for in the seminar, and then let Jesus share with you what he is most grateful for.)

C. OPTIONAL REFLECTION QUESTIONS

1. How would you pray with someone who has lost his or her best friend?

2. What helped you or another to grieve for a person's death and to grow from that experience?

3. What mistakes have you seen in how others have related to someone who was grieving over a death?

4. How do you feel you are connected or related to a person who has died?

D. OPTIONAL SUGGESTED READINGS

Scriptures (see Appendix B, "Scripture Prayer Helps")

John 11:1–44: Jesus grieves for his dead friend Lazarus and then Jesus prays for Lazarus.

1 Corinthians 13: All other things may pass away, but love never ends.

Romans 8:35–39: Nothing can separate us from the love of Christ, not even death.

1 Thessalonians 5:16–18: Rejoice and give thanks always because through Christ's death we have eternal life.

John 14:1–4: Jesus goes ahead of us to prepare a place for us in his Father's house.

Healing Life's Hurts, by Dennis and Matthew Linn (Ramsey, N.J.: Paulist Press, 1978). Praying for healing of hurts through the five stages of forgiveness. Elisabeth Kübler-Ross first developed the idea of the five stages in her work with dying patients as she observed their process of coming to accept death. This book proposes that death is the deepest hurt, and that we work through other hurts in a similar way as we walk with Jesus toward the final stage of forgiveness: gratitude for what has happened because of the new life that has come from it.

How To Pray for Spiritual Growth: A Practical Handbook of Inner Healing, by Theodore Dobson (Ramsey, N.J.: Paulist Press, 1982). Ten different ways to pray that will foster healing and spiritual growth, e.g., Cleansing the Imagination, Intellect, and Will; The Prayer of Quiet and Listening to God; Journal-Keeping; Forgiveness; Religious Imagery; Seeing Christ in the Events of Our Lives; Seeing Ourselves in the Events of Christ's Life.

Journal of Christian Healing, published by the Institute for Christian Healing, 103 Dudley Ave., Narberth, Pa. 19072. Semi-annual journal which integrates the findings of psychotherapy and of healing prayer. Includes articles on the practical aspects of how to pray for healing.

The Transformation of the Inner Man, by John and Paula Sandford (So. Plainfield, N.J.: Bridge, 1982). Comprehensive book on inner healing as the transformation of our deepest self into the likeness of Christ. (Note: Rev. and Mrs. Sandford are coming from an evangelical tradition which has a different understanding of the effects of original sin from our own Roman Catholic tradition. The evangelical tradition emphasizes the fallenness of human nature, while our tradition emphasizes our innate goodness, however flawed by the fall. While we do not share all of the Sandfords' assumptions about human nature and original sin, we do recommend this book for its fine chapters on specific areas of healing, e.g., sexual hurts.)

Note: If you wish to learn more about healing ministry and the dying, we recommend the video or audio tape series *Dying To Live: Spiritual Care For the Dying and Their Families,* by Bill and Jean Carr and Frs. Dennis and Matthew Linn, S.J., and the book upon which this series is based, *Healing the Dying,* by Mary Jane Linn, Dennis Linn and Matthew Linn (Ramsey, N.J.: Paulist Press, 1979). See the Appendix for information on where to order video and audio tapes. If you wish to learn more about prayer for the deceased, see the suggested readings for Lesson 10, "Tradition and Steps of Praying For the Deceased" and Lesson 11, "The Deceased Most Needing Prayer."

THEME 3: HEALING THE GREATEST HURT

Summary

What is the greatest hurt you have suffered or may have to face? In a study of hurtful and stressful situations, Dr. Holmes found that although conflict with in-laws was hurtful, going to jail was twice as hurtful, getting divorced three times as hurtful, and losing your spouse to death four times as hurtful.[1] Though each of these hurtful situations involves loss and therefore grief, perhaps the greatest hurt and therefore the greatest grief occurs in the loss of a loved one.

Lesson 9, "Healing Through Grieving," speaks about the physical, emotional, spiritual and social implications of unresolved grief. For instance, as regards physical implications, because unresolved grief lowers the immunity system which ordinarily fights off illness, widows and widowers have an illness rate sixteen times as great as the general population in the year after the death of their loved one. As regards emotional implications, psychiatrist Dr. Lindemann states that the amount of unresolved grief of patients entering mental hospitals is six times that of the national average.[2] We became convinced of the importance of grieving after being asked to pray with seven people with serious problems (alcoholism, homosexuality, etc.). We found, in five of the seven cases, that their emotional problems began shortly after the death of a close friend or a loved one. As we invited these people in prayer to grieve with Jesus and their loved one, the emotional problem also began to resolve.

If grieving with Jesus and the deceased in prayer is so important, than how do you do it? Lesson 10, "Traditions and Steps of Praying for the Deceased," shares the scriptural and later Christian tradition of this prayer and also exemplifies, through a short excerpt, a simple way to pray. Lesson 11, "The Deceased Most Needing Prayer," speaks about who, besides loved ones, can be helped by such prayer. Since healing can happen to you and the deceased any time more love is given or received, it is especially healing to pray with Jesus and those whom you may have hurt or those who may have hurt you (i.e., suicides, stillbirths, abortions, miscarriages, ancestors of past generations).

Lesson 12, "Prayer with Diane for Healing Abortion," includes a 22-minute prayer excerpt with Diane about nine years after her abortion. Diane, who had to be hospitalized in a mental institution shortly after her abortion, wonders how the "baby that I killed could ever want to be a part of me." Perhaps as you enter the healing prayer with Diane, you will discover how Jesus would lead you to pray similarly or differently with Diane or someone else experiencing grief.[3]

---

1. Thomas Holmes and Richard Rahe, "The Social Readjustment Scale," *Journal of Psychosomatic Research,* 11, (April 1967), 213–218.

2. Erich Lindemann, "Grief and Grief Management: Some Reflections," *The Journal of Pastoral Care,* 3 (September 1976), 198–207.

3. See *Healing the Greatest Hurt,* by Dennis & Matthew Linn, S.J. and Sheila Fabricant (to be published in 1985 by Paulist Press) for reading to accompany Theme 3.

THEME 3: HEALING THE GREATEST HURT
Lesson 9: Healing through grieving

I. Group Meeting

A. COMMON OPENING PRAYER AND SONG
(5 minutes)

B. FOR THOSE WHO ARE CONTINUING FROM LESSON 8:
INTRODUCTORY SHARING *(15 minutes)*

Share with your companion what has touched you most during the seminar thus far.

FOR THOSE WHO ARE BEGINNING THE SEMINAR WITH THIS SESSION *(15 minutes)*

Take time for all present to introduce themselves and to share what they hope for from this seminar. If the group is small, all present might also share what they do or what gives them life. The group leader might begin and then go around in a circle.

C. VIDEO OR AUDIO TAPE:
"Healing Through Grieving"
(30 minutes)

What are some of the most difficult situations that you have to face?

1. For most people, the most difficult situations are ones that involve grieving over a loss, e.g., loss of a job, loss of health, loss of a loved one, etc.

2. When the process of grieving is inhibited, unresolved grief can have harmful physical, emotional, spiritual and social effects upon us.

- Physical effects, e.g., depression of the immune system.
- Emotional effects, e.g., study of psychiatric patients, teenagers with illegitimate pregnancies, incidence of divorce among couples who have lost a child.

- Spiritual effects: grief may bring us closer to God or drive us further away from God, e.g., patients at Wohl Clinic vs. retreatants, C.S. Lewis and the death of his wife.
- Social effects, e.g., Khomeini, Martin Luther King, sister who works in the Tijuana prison.

3. The hurt of losing a loved one can become a blessing if we let God love us in the midst of our hurt (e.g., death of Matt's and Dennis' two-year-old brother).

4. The test for healthy grieving is to ask ourselves, "Is the love between me and the deceased continuing to deepen? Can I extend this love to others and form new friendships?" We can be healed of unresolved grief when we re-experience our bond of love with the person who has died and when we know that through Jesus we can continue to give and receive love with that person forever (e.g., Lisa and her grandmother).

Closing Prayer

(The Closing Prayer for each lesson invites you to pray for some aspect of Jesus' healing love. The prayers ask you to imagine with all your senses, but visual images are stressed more than sound, touch, smell or taste. Each person is unique in the use of imagination, and some people can picture things easily while others say they "Never see anything." Feel free to use your imagination in whatever way is most comfortable for you, e.g., through the senses of hearing or touch rather than through visual images.

You may find that you need a longer time for the Closing Prayer than is given on the tape. If so, the group leader might wish to lead the group through the prayer after the tape is over, allowing longer silences for each part of the prayer.)

Receiving Jesus' love through a deceased person who loved us.

- Let Jesus remind you of the deceased person who loved you the most (e.g., Lisa and her grandmother). Who is the person you miss the most? With Jesus, recall that person.
- Picture that person in Jesus' heart and experience how Jesus loves that person. Take a few deep breaths and experience Jesus' love passing into that person and filling him or her.
- Recall for a moment what you miss most about that person, a time when he or she especially loved you.
- Now enter into Jesus' heart, and as Jesus' love is filling that deceased person, let that person embrace you. Breathe in Jesus' love as it flows through that person and into you. Let yourself be filled in any ways you miss that person and in any empty places inside yourself.
- Ask Jesus how he wishes to continue to have your deceased loved one in your life (e.g., a special way he wants that person to intercede for you, situations when he wants the two of you to be in his heart and draw strength from each other, a way he invites you to let go of that person and place him or her more deeply in Jesus' heart). Tell Jesus what you need from him and how you especially want both you and the deceased to come closer to Jesus in the future.
- Thank Jesus for how he cares for both you and your deceased loved one and how he holds both of you in his heart.

D. SILENT REFLECTION (3 minutes)

Quiet time to get in touch with what moved you most in today's tape and prayer.

E. GUIDED JOURNALING (10 minutes)

1. Write down what is in your heart. Write as if you were writing a love letter to your best friend—Jesus—sharing what you feel most deeply. Don't worry about having the "right" words, but only try to share your heart.

2. Now get in touch with Jesus' response to you, as he is already speaking to you within. You might do this by asking what are the most loving words that you could hear in response, or perhaps by imagining that what you have just written is a note to you from the person you love most, and you want to respond to that person in the most loving possible words.

3. Write Jesus' response. Perhaps it will be just one word or one sentence. You can be sure that anything you write which helps you to know more clearly that you are loved is not just your own thoughts or imagination but is really what Jesus wants to say to you.

4. One or two people in the group might want to share what they have written with the whole group.

F. COMPANION SHARING
(5 minutes minimum for each person to share)

Share with your companion what moved you most in today's tape and prayer. You may wish to use your last few minutes to share with each other what you most want from Jesus and to pray with each other for it.

(If you are beginning the seminar with this session, you may wish to share and pray with the person next to you. At the next session, you will be asked to choose a prayer companion for the rest of the course.)

G. GROUP SHARING (15 minutes)

Share with the whole group what moved you most in today's tape and prayer.

H. CLOSING SNACK AND CELEBRATION

An open-ended time to enjoy each other and to continue sharing.

II. Home Experiences

A. DAILY HEALING PRAYER (10 minutes)

You may wish to use one of the following prayers. Feel free to repeat the same prayer for as many days as you wish, to return to a prayer from a previous lesson, or to pray in some other way.

1. *Session's Closing Prayer*

Return to any moment in the session's closing prayer that moved you. You may wish to pray this prayer with other deceased persons who are in Jesus' heart.

2. *Prayer for Healing Grief*

Recall the deceased person you miss the most. Tell Jesus about that person's death and how you miss him or her. Watch what Jesus says or does with you and that person.

3. *Gratitude Prayer*

With Jesus, make a list of your friends and relatives who have died. Let Jesus show you what you have received from each one. Join Jesus in thanking the Father.

4. *Embrace Prayer*

(Before we can face our own hurts or reach out to heal another, we need to know that we are loved. If what you are most in touch with is your need to experience God's love for you, you may wish to pray this prayer for as many days as needed until you feel filled.)

See Jesus standing before you or seated in a rocking chair. See him open his arms and invite you to him. Go to him, letting him hold you and perhaps rock you in the chair. Feel his arms around you and let yourself be loved as if you were a small child in its father's arms. (You may want to pray in a similar way with the Father, or with Mary as your mother, or join Jesus with a deceased person who loves you. Perhaps you will better be able to experience love by seeing yourself as the one embracing, e.g., picture yourself holding a child with Jesus. Or, you might want to pray this prayer at Eucharist, letting Jesus hold you in his arms as you receive Communion.)

5. *Contemplation in Action Prayer*

Soak yourself in the love which you and Jesus have for a deceased person and which Jesus and the deceased have for you. Ask Jesus whom he and the deceased want to love through you, perhaps a person close to the deceased or perhaps some other person who needs love. Spend 10 minutes doing something loving for that person.

B. DAILY JOURNAL *(5 minutes; see Appendix A, "Journaling: Writing a Love Letter")*

Review your prayer or day and write briefly, sharing with Jesus where you felt the most growth or where you felt the most longing for healing. Then listen as Jesus shares with you how he sees your prayer or day, and write his response. (Perhaps you may wish to share with Jesus what gift you have received from a deceased person, and let Jesus share with you how he has loved you through that person.)

C. OPTIONAL REFLECTION QUESTIONS

*(For group sharing or
personal reflection at home.)*

1. When have you experienced grieving? What effects did it have on you physically, emotionally, spiritually, socially, etc.?

2. What helps you to move through grieving?

3. When have you experienced a gift coming out of grieving (e.g., Matt's experience of his brother's death)?

4. Which deceased person do you miss the most? How would you like Jesus to be for you as that person was?

5. What problems (physical, emotional, spiritual) trouble you the most? Did any of these problems begin after the death of a loved one?

6. What social problems in the world might be related to grieving (e.g., Khomeini) and what social changes might be related to forgiveness and healing of grief (e.g., Martin Luther King)?

D. OPTIONAL SUGGESTED READING

See *Healing the Greatest Hurt,* by Dennis and Matthew Linn, S.J. and Sheila Fabricant (to be published in 1985 by Paulist Press) for reading to accompany Theme 3.

Scriptures

John 19:25–27: While dying on the cross, Jesus invites Mary and John into a new relationship of mother and son.

John 20:11–18: The risen Jesus tells Mary not to cling to him because he is going to "my Father and your Father."

John 21: Jesus appears to his disciples after his death, continuing his relationship with them.

A Grief Observed, by C.S. Lewis (New York: Bantam, 1961). C.S. Lewis' account of how he rediscovered a loving God as he worked through the process of grieving for his wife.

Good Grief, by Granger Westberg (Philadelphia: Fortress, 1962). Describes what happens to us whenever we lose someone or something important.

When Someone Dies, by Edgar Jackson (Philadelphia: Fortress, 1971). Presents grief not as an enemy, but rather as a process that can lead to healthful recovery from loss.

The Will of God, by Leslie Weatherhead (Nashville: Abingdon, 1944). What do we mean when we say that something is "the will of God"? It is important that we understand this correctly if we are to find a loving God in the midst of grief.

In Memoriam, by Henri Nouwen (Notre Dame: Ave Maria, 1980). The author shares his experience of the death of his mother.

On Death and Dying, by Elisabeth Kübler-Ross (New York: Macmillan, 1969). Describes the five emotional stages a person goes through in preparing for death, culminating in acceptance. These same five stages can be applied to the process of forgiving God, ourselves and others for any hurt or loss (see *Healing Life's Hurts: Healing Memories Through the Five Stages of Forgiveness,* by Dennis and Matthew Linn).

The Bereaved Parent, by Harriet Sarnoff Schiff (New York: Penguin, 1977). See especially the chapter on "Bereavement and Marriage," discussing the stress placed upon marriages by the loss of a child.

"The Social Readjustment Scale," by Thomas Holmes and Richard Rahe, *Journal of Psychosomatic Research,* Vol. 11, April 1967, pp. 213–218. Study of the stress levels produced by different kinds of situations. The most stressful life events involve loss, especially loss of a loved one as in divorce or death.

"How the Mind Heals," by Alan Anderson, *Psychology Today,* Vol. 16, No. 2, December 1982, pp. 50–56. Includes a report of research at Mount Sinai Hospital in New York, studying the relationship between bereavement and activity of the immune system.

"Grief and Grief Management: Some Reflections," by Erich Lindemann, *The Journal of Pastoral Care,* Vol. 30, No. 3, September 1976, pp. 198–207. Discusses the nature of grief, in its healthy and unhealthy forms. Includes statistics on the unusually high number of serious losses in the life histories of psychiatric patients.

"Adolescent Mourning Reactions to Infant and Fetal Loss," by Nancy Heller Horowitz, *Social Casework,* Vol. 59, No. 9, November 1978, pp. 551– 59. Study of adolescents with two or more illegitimate pregnancies. In fifty percent of these cases, the girl had suffered a serious loss prior to one of the pregnancies. In twenty percent of the cases the loss was of a parent—in all but one case, the father. This study suggests that in some cases illegitimate pregnancy may be an expression of unresolved grief, i.e., an effort to replace the lost loved one.

"Blessed Are Those Who Mourn: An Exploration of Political Grief," by Michael B. Russell, *Sojourners,* Vol. 11, No. 1, January 1982, pp. 24–26. A whole group of people or subculture can be weighed down and emotionally paralyzed by unresolved grief, as in the case of a community of millworkers suffering from brown lung disease.

"Despair Work," by Joanna Macy, *Evolutionary Blues,* No. 1. (Reprints available from *Evolutionary Blues,* Box 4448, Arcata, Cal. 95521.) We may carry buried despair over the hurts suffered by our world (e.g., nuclear weapons, environmental destruction) just as we may carry buried grief for more immediately personal hurts. We can find new life and strength as we face and work through our despair, just as we can find new life and strength by grieving a loss.

"Grief and Inner Healing," by Phoebe Cranor (Pecos, N.M.: Dove Publications, Leaflet #12). When we experience the loss of a person, job, health, etc., our grief is not only for the thing lost but also for the part of ourselves represented by what we have lost. Our griefs of the present can be healed more easily when we let Jesus show us what part of ourselves feels as though it has died along with what we have lost and how we may have buried unhealed griefs of the past in the same area of our being. As Jesus breathes his life into this wounded part of us, we can move through grieving for our present loss.

THEME 3: HEALING THE GREATEST HURT

Lesson 10: Tradition and steps of praying for the deceased

I. Group Meeting

A. COMMON OPENING PRAYER AND SONG (5 minutes)

B. INTRODUCTORY SHARING (10 minutes)

Share with your companion what touched you most (in your prayer or outside of it) during the previous week. (Perhaps you might wish to share who is the deceased person who has gifted you the most.) What are you most grateful for and how do you need Jesus' help?

C. VIDEO OR AUDIO TAPE:

"Tradition and Steps of Praying for the Deceased" (30 minutes)

What does Christian tradition say about prayer for the deceased, and how do we go about this kind of prayer?

1. Our tradition of prayer for the deceased goes back to the Old Testament (Bar 3, Dan 9:16ff, 2 Mac 12) and the New Testament (2 Tim 1:18, 1 Cor 12:12, 1 Cor 13:13).

2. Deuteronomy 18:10–11 and 1 Samuel 28 state that we may not consult the deceased or contact them through mediums. In our understanding of prayer for the deceased, we go through Jesus rather than a medium, and we love and forgive the deceased rather than consult or summon them. Unlike a séance, in our prayer we do not call the deceased to be physically present to us but only spiritually present to us in Jesus' heart, to experience his love and forgiveness.

3. Recent developments in theology encourage us to see purgatory as more like a hospital than a prison.

4. Our transition from this world to the next might be compared to the birth of a child (e.g., Jn 3:3). Those who loved us here and who drew us into the heart of Jesus can continue to help us grow in giving and receiving love, just as a mother who loved and nourished her baby in the womb can continue to love it after birth.

5. How do we pray for the deceased? There are three steps (e.g., Matt's prayer with Sandy):

- Heal our relationship with Jesus, by letting Jesus love us and grieve with us, just as he grieved with Martha and Mary for Lazarus.
- Heal our relationship with the deceased. In this step we unbind the deceased by giving and receiving love and forgiveness.
- Give thanks to God for what has happened in our prayer and for all the ways he will bring us new life that will continue to fill the emptiness left by our loved one's death.

Closing Prayer

Becoming one in Jesus with a deceased person.

- Let Jesus show you the deceased person whom he wants you to pray for and love, and whom he wants to love through your heart.
- See Jesus bring that person to you. See him put his arm around you and that person, and bring you together so you can all feel all the love in his heart.
- Take in from Jesus whatever you need, especially any way you miss that deceased person. Let Jesus be there for you in the way that person was there. See how Jesus rejoices that he can be for you some of what that person was for you,

and that you have a hunger for him you never had before.

- Breathe Jesus in until you feel his eagerness to love the person who is deceased. Then let Jesus' prayer, "Abba, Father" be in your heart, and let the Father's love flow through Jesus into you, and through you into the deceased person. Offer that person any forgiveness he or she might need from you, any prayer for healing, or any other way you can say, "Jesus and I love you." Breathe Jesus' love into the person until you see him or her become as peaceful and joyful as Jesus, and until you sense that he or she feels loved by the Father and a part of Jesus' family forever.
- Let Jesus and the deceased person offer you the perfect love of the Father and welcome you into the Father's family. Breathe in the love, forgiveness and healing which Jesus and the deceased person offer you, until you share their peace, security and joy.
- When you know what it is to be one in Jesus in the Father's family and to give and receive love with the deceased person with the heart of Jesus, stand up and hug the person next to you in the same way you would like to hug the deceased person you've just given to Jesus.

D. SILENT REFLECTION (3 minutes)

Quiet time to get in touch with what moved you most in today's tape and prayer.

E. GUIDED JOURNALING (10 minutes)
(See page **88**.)

F. COMPANION SHARING (5 minutes minimum for each person to share)

Share with your companion what moved you most in today's tape. End by sharing what you are most grateful for and how you need Jesus' help.

G. COMPANION PRAYER (5 minutes minimum of prayer for each person)

Pray for your companion for about 5 minutes, either silently or aloud in your own words. Give thanks for what your companion is most grateful for and ask for whatever your companion most needs. Then let your companion pray for you.

H. GROUP SHARING (15 minutes)

Share with the whole group what moved you most in today's tape and prayer.

I. CLOSING SNACK AND CELEBRATION

An open-ended time to enjoy one another and continue sharing.

II. Home Experiences

A. DAILY HEALING PRAYER (10 minutes)

You may wish to use one of the following prayers. Feel free to repeat the same prayer for as many days as you wish, to return to a prayer from a previous lesson, or to pray in some other way.

1. *Session's Closing Prayer*

Return to any moment in the session's closing prayer that moved you. You may wish to pray this prayer with another deceased person whom Jesus wants you to pray for and love.

2. *Healing Relationship with Jesus*
- Join Jesus as he loves Martha and Mary and all those who weep for Lazarus.
- Ask Jesus to help you recall a time when a loved one died.
- Let Jesus love you and grieve with you for your deceased loved one. Tell him how you miss the person and are grateful for the person.
- With Martha and Mary, forgive Jesus for any way you feel he wasn't there, and allow Jesus to be with you in any way you need him now.

3. *Healing the Relationship with the Deceased*
- Ask Jesus to help you remember a deceased person whom you need to be reconciled with.
- Join Jesus in healing and unbinding the deceased person.
- Tell Jesus and the deceased person what you wish you had said and done.
- Look at how much Jesus loves and wants to heal both you and the deceased person. As you move into the depth of his healing love, see if Jesus leads the deceased person to say or do anything for you that will bring love and forgiveness to you and closeness to Jesus.
- Invite Jesus, Mary and the Father into your longing for the deceased and let them be for

you everything and more that the deceased person was. When you are totally filled with their love, breathe it out upon the deceased person.
- Let Jesus hug both of you and let him tell you how he wants you to continue to love each other in ways that bring you both closer to him forever.

4. *Giving Thanks for New Life*
Thank the Lord for any ways in which new life has come to you through the death of a loved one (e.g., a deeper prayer life, reaching out to make new friends, getting involved in new activities, a sense of that person's intercession for you, caring for those he or she left behind, etc.).

5. *Embrace Prayer*
(See page **89**.)

7. *Prayer for a Deceased Person*
With Jesus get in touch with your love for a deceased person for whom you wish to pray. Write out your prayer for that person. At the next session you may wish to share this prayer with your companion. Perhaps on another day you may wish to do this same kind of prayer, except this time write how Jesus is praying to his Father for that deceased person.

B. DAILY JOURNAL *(5 minutes)*
Review your prayer or day and write briefly, sharing with Jesus where you felt the most growth or where you felt the most longing for healing. Then listen as Jesus shares with you how he sees your prayer or day, and write his response. (Perhaps you may wish to share with Jesus what helps or hinders you in loving a deceased person, and see what Jesus says or does.)

C. OPTIONAL REFLECTION QUESTIONS
(For group sharing or
personal reflection at home.)

1. When have you experienced prayer for the deceased to be helpful and what made it so?
2. When have you been angry at God? Why? What helped you?
3. Have you ever felt at the death of someone that Jesus wasn't there? What helped?
4. It's never too late to love and forgive. When have you experienced loving and forgiving someone more after that person's death than before it? What helped?

5. Which deceased person who hurt you is Jesus asking you to love and forgive? How is he asking you to begin?
6. Which deceased person whom you have hurt is Jesus asking you to love and ask for forgiveness? How is he asking you to begin?

D. OPTIONAL SUGGESTED READING
Scriptures (see Appendix B, "Scripture Prayer Helps")
John 11:1–44: Jesus prays for his dead friend, Lazarus.
2 Timothy 1:18: Paul asks for prayers for the deceased Onesiphorus.
1 Samuel 28: Saul is in trouble for consulting the deceased Samuel.
Deuteronomy 18:11: We are forbidden to consult the deceased.
1 Corinthians 12: We are all unique parts of one body.
1 Corinthians 15: Both the living and the dead are part of the one body of Christ.
1 Corinthians 13: Love bonds us together beyond death.
John 3:3: Jesus compares entering the Kingdom of God to being born again.

Afterlife: The Other Side of Dying, by Morton Kelsey (Ramsey, N.J.: Paulist Press, 1979). What happens after we die, and why a belief in afterlife is important for our spiritual and psychological health. (Note: While we recommend this book in general, we differ with the position Dr. Kelsey takes in Chapter 12, pages 235–236 where he says that "reincarnation is a possible occurrence" and a possible though inadequate explanation for "memories of past lives." The questions which Dr. Kelsey himself raises about reincarnation in this chapter are good ones, which we would underline. Our own position is the "memories" of past lives are never actually memories of our own experiences, but usually the experiences of deceased persons with whom we are in relationship through the body of Christ.)
The Everlasting Now, by George Maloney (Notre Dame: Ave Maria, 1980). An exploration of death, heaven, hell, purgatory, the mystical body of Christ, the resurrection and related concepts, based on the author's study of theology and Scripture. Presents life, death and life after death as

stages in our development toward full maturity as unique and loving persons.

All Hallows' Eve, by Charles Williams (Grand Rapids: William B. Eerdmans, 1948), and *Descent into Hell,* by Charles Williams (Grand Rapids: William B. Eerdmans, 1937). Both of these novels by Williams present in fictional form the reality of the spiritual world and how it impinges on our world, especially through our ongoing relationship with the deceased.

Healing the Dying, by Mary Jane Linn, Dennis Linn and Matthew Linn (Ramsey, N.J.: Paulist Press, 1979), Chapter 8, "Peace. As the Father Sends Me, So I Send You." How we can receive healing by praying for a deceased loved one and receiving the love that person wishes to send us. Based on Matt's experience of praying for his deceased and beloved uncle, Fr. Joe Linn, and includes a theological explanation of prayer for the deceased.

" 'One Body in Christ': Death and the Communion of Saints," by Kallistos Ware, *Sobornost,* Vol. 3, No. 2, 1981, pp. 179–191. We can pray for the deceased because the communion of saints is a communion of prayer, in which death is no longer an impassable barrier.

Life After Life, by Raymond Moody (Covington, Ga.: Mockingbird Books, 1975). Dr. Moody interviewed over one thousand people who reported near death experiences with over fifteen common elements, including being met by a deceased loved one and a loving Being of Light. While this research is not scientific proof that love endures beyond death, it shows that many near death often meet such a deep love that they are no longer afraid of dying.

Reflections on Life After Life, by Raymond Moody (New York: Bantam, 1977). Dr. Moody reports that several people having near death experiences saw a "realm of bewildered spirits . . . bound to some particular object, person or habit. . . . These dulled spirits were to be there only until they solved whatever problem or difficulty was keeping them in that perplexed state" (p. 18). While not scientifically proving a purgatory, it does indicate that people near death may become aware of a need for purification after death by at least some of the deceased.

THEME 3: HEALING THE GREATEST HURT

Lesson 11: The deceased most needing prayer

I. Group Meeting

A. COMMON OPENING PRAYER
AND SONG *(5 minutes)*

B. INTRODUCTORY SHARING *(10 minutes)*

If you have written a prayer for a deceased loved one, as suggested in Prayer #6 of the previous week's Home Experience, you may wish to share it at this time. Or share with your companion what touched you most (in your prayer or outside of it) during the previous week. What are you most in touch with that you need from Jesus?

C. VIDEO OR AUDIO TAPE:

"The Deceased Most Needing Prayer"
(30 minutes)

If it's so important to pray for the deceased, who are the ones that especially need our prayers?

1. The person we miss the most.
2. A person we hurt or who hurt us.
3. Those who committed suicide. We see a person who commits suicide as emotionally ill rather than as deliberately rebelling against God (e.g., a person jumping from a burning building).
4. Miscarried, aborted and stillborn babies. Praying for a deceased baby is not only important for the family (e.g., anorexia nervosa, nurse with depression), but also for the baby. Recent research has shown that babies remember things, including experiences in the womb. Thus they need Jesus' love and healing.
5. Ancestors. Because the unhealed hurts of parents may be lived out in their children, it is important to pray for ancestors (e.g., Matt's Irish priest friend). It is also important to pray for our ancestors because when, in prayer, we give and receive love with our ancestors we can grow in all the ways they were gifted (e.g., Matt and Dennis in Ireland).

Closing Prayer

Asking Jesus to send his love back through our family line.

- Get in touch with Mary's love for Jesus and how she would do anything for him. See how lovingly Mary looks into Jesus' eyes.
- Then let Mary look into your own eyes. Breathe out any ways you have received hurts from your own mother, and breathe in Mary's perfect mother's love. Mary was given to each of us at the foot of the cross, so breathe in her love and breathe out any fears, hurts, resentments or other bondage that may have come to you through your mother's side of the family.
- When you feel filled with Mary's love, breathe it out toward your mother, especially into those parts of her that are also a part of you. Let Mary's love fill in any wounded places in your mother.
- As you breathe Mary's love into your mother, see it flow backward through her to your grandmother, your great-grandmother and all the way through your family line, and to any of the people who may have hurt any of your ancestors. Ask Jesus to find the faces of those ancestors you don't know, and to breathe his love into them.
- Ask Jesus to free you from any way you have inherited hurt or bondage, and to give his love to all the deceased in your family in any way they are wounded and never received that love.

D. SILENT REFLECTION *(3 minutes)*

Quiet time to get in touch with what moved you most in today's tape and prayer.

E. GUIDED JOURNALING *(10 minutes)*

(See page **88**.)

F. COMPANION SHARING *(5 minutes minimun for each person to share)*

Share with your companion what moved you most in today's tape and prayer. End by sharing what you are most grateful for and how you need Jesus' help.

G. COMPANION PRAYER
(5 minutes minimum of prayer for each person)

Pray for your companion for about 5 minutes, either silently or aloud in your own words. Give thanks for what your companion is most grateful for and ask for whatever your companion most needs. Then let your companion pray for you.

H. GROUP SHARING *(15 minutes)*

Share with the whole group what moved you most in today's tape and prayer.

I. CLOSING SNACK AND CELEBRATION

II. Home Experiences

A. DAILY HEALING PRAYER *(10 minutes)*

You may wish to use one of the following prayers. Feel free to repeat the same prayer for as many days as you wish, to return to a prayer from a previous lesson, or to pray in some other way.

1. *Session's Closing Prayer*

Return to any moment in the session's closing prayer that moved you. You may wish to pray this prayer with your father and his side of the family.

2. *Mother or Father's Prayer for a Deceased Baby* (Stillborn, Miscarried or Aborted)

Read Mark 10:13–16, where Jesus asks for the children to come to him.

- *Forgiveness.* See Mary and Jesus holding the child and offering it to you. With them, hold the baby and ask forgiveness from Jesus and from the child for any way in which you failed to love the child. (Catholics who have been involved in an abortion should also make use of

the sacrament of reconciliation as part of this step of receiving forgiveness.) Then take a minute to see what Jesus or the child says or does in response to you. With Jesus and the child, forgive anyone else who may have hurt the child (doctors, other family members, etc.)—anyone who, even unknowingly, didn't nourish this new life. Perhaps you or another even experience anger at God for sending the child at the "wrong" time or for taking the child.

- *Baptizing into Jesus' Family.* Now choose a name for the child and let Jesus wash away all hurt by baptizing the child into his family. Say with Jesus, "I baptize you (name), in the name of the Father and of the Son and of the Holy Spirit." Feel the water cleansing and making all things new.

- *Prayer.* Say a prayer for the child to receive all the love that only Jesus and Mary can give. When you really want the child to be eternally happy even more than you want it to be alive again, place the child in the arms of Jesus and Mary and see them do all the things that you can't do.

- *Mass.* If you are Catholic, have a Mass said for the child and, if possible, attend it or another Mass. As you receive Communion, let Jesus' love and forgiving blood flow through you to the child and to all other deceased members of your family tree.

3. *Prayer for a Person Who Has Committed Suicide or Who Was Difficult To Love*

Read Luke 23:39–43, where Jesus gives paradise to the good thief. Stand on Calvary with Jesus and forgive the good thief.

- Ask Jesus about the pressures that were upon the person you are praying for. Ask Jesus to also show you the good that he saw in the person in the last moments, when others saw only a "condemned thief" or a suicide.

- We are called upon only to forgive, and to leave judgment in the hands of the merciful Shepherd who seeks out every last sheep. Stay at the foot of the cross until you can see your deceased person take the place of the good thief on the cross. See yourself in the heart of Jesus on the cross, loved by the Father and extending forgiveness to the good thief. With Jesus, forgive all in this person's life until you can say Jesus' words, "This day you shall be with me in paradise." Want all that Jesus wants for this person, until you can release him or her into Jesus' hands. Know that any forgiveness you are able to give must come from God and that it is only a shadow of his mercy.

- Ask forgiveness for any way in which you feel that you failed to give this person life, and see Jesus holding the person and breathing that life into him or her now, through your prayer. Do this until you can sense that the one you hurt is able to say, "Jesus." Let the person join Jesus in looking at you with love and in giving you life too.

4. *Heart Prayer for the Deceased*
- *Forgiving God and the Deceased and Letting Them Forgive Us.* Ask Jesus to make the deceased person you are praying for present in his heart. Tell Jesus and the person how you miss him or her and wish you had been able to love more. Share what you wish you had said or done before the death. Share also your anger at God for the way the death occurred, the hardships caused by the death and your own feelings of being abandoned. If you are ready to forgive God, share with him your sorrow at any distance that has been between you and him since the death. Let Jesus share with you how he and the deceased forgive you and love you. Maybe Jesus will lead the deceased person in sharing with you how he or she may need forgiveness for having hurt you. If there is anything that you need to forgive, extend this forgiveness.
- *Receiving Love.* Ask Jesus, the Father or Mary to love you in those parts of yourself that are still lonely for the deceased person. Breathe in this love and breathe out all within you that longs for the person.
- *Releasing the Deceased To Be Loved.* Place your hand on the heart of Jesus and pray for him to love and free the deceased in all the ways that you cannot do so. When you sense Jesus' love healing and freeing the person, take away your hand and let him or her remain even more deeply in the heart of Jesus.

5. *Praying for the Deceased at Eucharist*

- *Forgiveness.* At the start of Mass, forgive the deceased person and God. Ask them to forgive you too.

- As you offer the Mass, let Jesus stand between you and the deceased person. Allow Jesus to draw you both closer to him in his one bread, one body.
- As you receive Communion, allow Jesus to fill you with his love in those parts of your being where you still miss the deceased person. Then, when you are filled with Jesus' love, ask that Jesus' blood flow back through you to cleanse the deceased person and your whole family lineage of any inherited weakness or occult bondage. (Curses, seals or ancestral occult involvement should be broken by the blood of Jesus three times.) Then watch Jesus' blood flow back to bond all the deceased to himself in an eternal covenant. End by releasing the deceased person into the everlasting care of Jesus.

(Often when curses, pacts and seals are enacted, they are repeated three times in mockery of the Trinity. They can be broken by receiving the Eucharist and sincerely praying three times, "In the name of Jesus Christ and through the power of his precious blood, I break all curses, pacts, seals or any other occult bondage and totally give myself to my Lord Jesus Christ.")

6. *Gratitude for Ancestry*
Ask Jesus to show you what positive characteristics, traits and attitudes have been handed down to you from your mother's ancestry and from your father's ancestry. With Jesus, thank the Father for these gifts. (At the next session, you may wish to share with your companion what Jesus has shown you.)

7. *Embrace Prayer*
(See page **89.**)

B. DAILY JOURNAL *(5 minutes)*
Review your prayer or day and write briefly, sharing with Jesus where you felt the most growth or where you felt the most longing for healing. Then listen as Jesus shares with you how he sees your prayer or day, and write his response. (Perhaps you may wish to share with Jesus how you think your ancestors need love, and see what Jesus says or does.)

C. OPTIONAL REFLECTION QUESTIONS
(For group sharing or personal reflection at home.)

1. Make a list of the deceased persons who may need your prayers, e.g., those you loved the most,

those you hurt or who hurt you, those easily forgotten (suicides, miscarried, aborted or stillborn babies, ancestors).

2. Have you noticed in yourself or in your family any physical, emotional or spiritual effects of unresolved grief for any of the above deaths?

3. What positive characteristics, traits and attitudes have been handed down to you from your mother's ancestry and from your father's ancestry?

4. What negative characteristics, traits and attitudes have been handed down to you from your mother's ancestry and from your father's ancestry?

5. What would you tell a person whose son or daughter has committed suicide and who wonders whether that child will be saved?

6. How would you pray with a woman who has had an abortion?

D. OPTIONAL SUGGESTED READINGS

Scriptures (See Appendix B, "Scripture Prayer Helps")

Leviticus 26:39–40: The Israelites can ask forgiveness for the sins of their fathers.

Daniel 9:20: Daniel confesses his sins and the sins of his ancestors. Gabriel hears the prayer.

Baruch 3:1–8: Prayer of the exiled Israelites to be freed from bondage to the sins of their ancestors.

Exodus 20:5: Sins of the father are handed down for four generations.

2 Maccabees 12:42–46: Judas Maccabeus prays for the deceased soldiers to be freed from their sins.

1 Corinthians 7:14: An unbeliever can be joined to the communion of saints through the prayer of a family member, his or her spouse.

Luke 7:11–17: Jesus prays for the dead son of the widow of Naim.

Luke 1:41: The baby in Elizabeth's womb knows the presence of Jesus and leaps for joy.

1 Corinthians 13: Love bonds us together beyond death.

1 Corinthians 12:12: We are all one body, connected together.

1 Corinthians 15:29: Baptism on behalf of the dead indicates some form of prayer for the deceased.

Healing the Family Tree, by Kenneth McAll (London: Sheldon Press, 1982). How prayer for the deceased, especially through the Eucharist, can free and heal the living. Discusses anorexia nervosa as related to a family history of abortion, miscarriage or stillbirth.

Your Inner Child of the Past, by Hugh Missildine (New York: Simon & Schuster, 1963). The attitudes and behaviors of parents live on in their children and continue to affect future generations.

Born To Win, by Muriel James and Dorothy Jongeward (Reading, Mass.: Addison-Wesley, 1981). We each have an inner "parent," formed by how our own parents related to us, and we may each be living out a "life script," based on patterns handed down to us by our family.

"Healing of an Abortion Through the Eucharist," by Sheila Fabricant, *Journal of Christian Healing,* Vol. 5, No. 1, Spring 1983, p. 52. Account of a woman who experienced a simulated labor during a Eucharist for her aborted child.

"Limbo," *New Catholic Encyclopedia,* Vol. 8, pp. 762–65. There is no official endorsement by the Roman Catholic Church for the doctrine of limbo.

"Life After Death," J.T. Ryan interviewing Monika Hellwig, *Sign,* April 1979, p. 35. How the word *"limbo,"* meaning margin in Latin, came to be mistakenly used to refer to a place where unbaptized babies dwelled. The original intention of theologians was to say that they could not answer the question of where deceased, unbaptized babies went, and therefore had to place this question in the margin (in "limbo").

"The Conditioning of the Human Fetus in Utero," by David K. Spelt, *Journal of Experimental Psychology,* Vol. 38, No. 3, June 1948, pp. 338–346. Classic experiment in which fetuses were conditioned to respond to a loud noise, thus demonstrating that the child in the womb can learn.

"The Embryology of Consciousness," by Andrew Feldmar, in *The Psychological Aspects of Abortion,* edited by David Mall and Walter F. Watts, (Washington, D.C.: University Press of America, 1979). Account of patients who tried to commit suicide at the same time each year—the same time when their mothers had tried to abort them while they were in the womb.

"Follow-up Study From Birth of the Effects of Prenatal Stresses," by D.H. Stott, *Develop. Med. Child Neurol.,* Vol. 15, 1973, pp. 770–787. Prolonged stress, especially marital discord, during pregnancy has the greatest negative effect upon the child after birth.

The Secret Life of the Unborn Child, by Thomas Verny (New York: Summit, 1981). Summary of current scientific knowledge of the sensitivity and awareness of the child in the womb. Page 76 describes the experiment referred to in this session, where a pregnant woman's fear that her unmoving child was in danger was communicated to her child and produced an immediate kicking reaction in the child.

"Maternal Emotionality During Pregnancy and Reproductive Outcome: A Review of the Literature," by Dimity B. Carlson and Richard C. Labarba, *International Journal of Behavioral Development,* Vol. 2, 1979, pp. 343–376. The incidence of stillbirth is greatest among women who conceived illegitimately and who have little or no support from their families.

"Science of Touch and Feeling Has a Great Import for Preborn," by S.N. Bauer, *St. Cloud Visitor,* Vol. 71, No. 24, Nov. 11, 1982, pp. 1 and 11. Account of lecture by Dr. Franz Veldman, on the importance of communicating love to the unborn child, through touch. (See also *Feeling & Healing Your Emotions,* by Conrad W. Baars (Plainfield, N.J.: Bridge, 1979), pp. 82–84. Dr. Baars summarizes Dr. Veldman's method of communicating with the fetus.)

"Maternal Reactions to Involuntary Fetal/Infant Death," by Larry G. Peppers and Ronald J. Knapp, *Psychiatry,* Vol. 43, May 1980, pp. 155–159. The grief experienced by mothers over miscarriage is as great as the grief they experience at the death of a newborn child.

Motherhood and Mourning: Perinatal Death, by Larry G. Peppers and Ronald J. Knapp (New York: Praeger Publishers, 1980). Account of maternal grief at the loss of a baby and of healthy ways for a mother to grieve after the death of a stillbirth, miscarriage, or newborn. Too often we assume that a mother after a stillbirth or miscarriage does not need to grieve, yet studies indicate emotional and physical grief reactions similar to those experienced by a mother after the death of any close loved one.

E. THINKING ABOUT THE FUTURE

On one or two days this week, you may wish to spend your prayer time praying over and writing your response to the following questions:

Do I want to continue this experience in some way after the course is finished?

If so, how?

For example, you may find that you might want to:

- Stop because of other commitments.
- Split up and start the course for others, perhaps at several different days and times.
- Have periodic gatherings, e.g., a future retreat, project or liturgy.
- Take the *Prayer Course for Healing Life's Hurts,* by Dennis and Matthew Linn, S.J. and Sheila Fabricant, if you have not already done so (available from Paulist Press; see Appendix E).
- Meet together to view the video tape series *Dying To Live: Spiritual Care for the Dying and Their Families,* with Bill and Jean Carr and Dennis and Matthew Linn, S.J. (These talks are also available in audio tape form, and are based on the book *Healing the Dying,* by Mary Jane Linn, Dennis Linn and Matthew Linn. Video-tapes, audio tapes and book are available from Paulist Press. See Appendix E for information on where to order.)
- Use the same course format and continue with tapes by other speakers, e.g., Jim Wheeler, S.J., *School for Spiritual Growth and Inner Healing,* 4204 San Ysidro Ave., Albuquerque, N.M. 87107. Also, ALU, 504 Antioch Lane, Ballwin, Mo. 63011, has tapes on prayer and healing by many speakers.
- Other suggestions?

THEME 3: HEALING THE GREATEST HURT

Lesson 12: Prayer with Diane for healing abortion

I. Group Meeting

A. COMMON OPENING PRAYER AND SONG (5 minutes)

B. INTRODUCTORY SHARING (10 minutes)

Share with your companion what touched you most (in your prayer or outside of it) during the previous week. (You may wish to share what positive characteristics, traits and attitudes have been handed down to you from your mother's ancestry and from your father's ancestry, as suggested in Prayer #6 of the previous week's Home Experiences.) What are you most grateful for and how do you need Jesus' help?

C. VIDEO OR AUDIO TAPE:

"Prayer with Diane for Healing Abortion" (30 minutes)

How would you pray with a person who has experienced the painful trauma of an abortion?

1. In praying for the death of a loved one, there are three steps: healing our relationship with Jesus, healing our relationship with the deceased, and giving thanks for the new life we've received. In our prayer with Diane, we focused on the second step of healing the relationship with the deceased, since Diane's deepest hurt from this experience is wondering if the baby she killed would ever want to have her as a mother.

2. Diane's abortion took place nine years before our prayer with her. When Diane came for prayer, she brought her newborn child, seven-week-old Sarah. Diane shared with us that she was so traumatized by the abortion that she had to be hospitalized in a mental institution afterward. She described the confusion and inadequacy she had felt as an illegitimately pregnant teenager, afraid she had disappointed both her parents and herself. At the time she had not understood the significance of abortion: "I didn't know much about abortion then. All I knew was that you got an abortion and you weren't pregnant anymore." Only afterward did Diane realize what she had done and she became filled with self-hatred. Her family was unable to offer her love and forgiveness at the time, and their reaction added to her burden of guilt. Diane's self-hatred led her to behave in self-destructive ways for the next several years, for example drug abuse, as a way of telling the world, "I'm ugly. I'm a horrible person and I don't deserve any goodness in my life." At times Diane would lash out at her parents, telling them, "I hate you. I hate you." Years later she realized that she was really saying, "I hate me." Before the prayer Diane told us, "I didn't realize that giving life was such a beautiful and wonderful thing. And I guess what hurts now . . . you know, I denied that . . . and how could this baby even want a part of me, the baby that I killed?"

3. Dennis begins the prayer with Diane by encouraging her to breathe out her self-hatred and her fear that her child would not want her as a mother, and to breathe in Jesus' love. Diane's most meaningful experience of giving and receiving love in the present is her baby Sarah, and so Dennis encourages Diane to let Jesus' love flow into her through Sarah.

4. When Diane is in touch with how God has loved her by giving her Sarah, Dennis asks her to get in touch with her aborted baby. Dennis suggests that Diane see Mary holding and loving that baby, just as Diane holds and loves Sarah. Diane is able to get in touch with her aborted child. She wants to hold that child and "to tell it I'm sorry." Dennis encourages Diane to ask Jesus to give her the aborted child and to let her hold it as closely as she holds Sarah.

5. Diane experiences Jesus giving the aborted child to her. Diane is deeply moved and begins to sob.

After several minutes she tells Dennis, "I felt as though my heart just sort of opened up to the baby that I didn't have. And I could just sort of pour this love over the baby. . . . And the baby, I could feel it love me back. And it was just as though we were passing our love back and forth to each other." Dennis invites Diane to remain with this experience for several more minutes, exchanging love with her child. Then Diane says, "I just have a deep, deep sense of peace and love with this child. Just happiness. To me it seems strange, but I also get a sense of what sex the child was." Dennis encourages Diane to ask her child what name it would like, and Diane senses that her child wants to be called "Joseph." Diane sees Jesus baptizing her child, as she and Dennis name the child Joseph. Dennis asks Diane if she wants Joseph to be present and intercede for her in some special way, and Diane answers: "Just knowing he loves me back . . . is all I need." Dennis closes the prayer by asking that Joseph will always be as close to Diane as Sarah is.

NOTE: The Catholic Church has taught that a person who dies without receiving baptism by water may still be saved by a "baptism of desire." Baptism of desire means desiring to be incorporated into Jesus as fully as happens through baptism. Most theologians believe infants dying without water baptism are not sent to limbo but given the chance to choose Jesus forever, i.e., a baptism of desire for the fullness of life in Jesus. In asking Jesus to baptize a deceased infant, we are asking Jesus to do whatever still needs to be done for that infant whether it be initiating baptism of desire or renewing it with a deeper celebration of Jesus' love offered through us. Ideally, as recommended by the Council of Trent, this prayer should be completed by a Eucharist in which we receive Communion and join Jesus praying for us and the deceased to draw closer to him forever. Eucharist is also an ideal time to give Jesus' love to others who may have been forgotten, such as the 3,500 children aborted daily in the United States. Especially at Eucharist the deceased are empowered with Christ's total forgiveness on Calvary. By receiving Christ's forgiveness for themselves and then extending that forgiveness toward all who have hurt them, the deceased are enabled to enter heaven, the state of loving the whole mystical body of Christ forever.

6. After the prayer, Diane shares her joy and surprise that Joseph would love her and want to be close to her. The forgiveness between Diane and Joseph had been instantaneous, as soon as Jesus placed Joseph on Diane, with "no questions asked."

7. Three months after the prayer, Diane shared with us how it had affected her life. She found that many other hurts which she had buried, e.g., her own experience of being abused as a child, began to surface. She was able to let Jesus heal these hurts also, as she shared them with friends who could pray with her. Diane believes that the hurt of her abortion was so deep that it had become a kind of inner blockage, preventing God's love from reaching any part of her. But when she saw that God's love and mercy are so great that he would love and forgive her even for an abortion, she was free to let him love and heal her other hurts also. Diane also stated that she continues to feel Joseph's presence and his care for herself and Sarah. When Sarah became sick and Diane felt tired and drained from caring for Sarah, Diane asked Joseph to intercede. Diane found this a source of strength and comfort, knowing that Joseph is with Jesus and that he cares for her and Sarah. Diane no longer feels that she is unworthy to be a mother because she killed her first baby. Now Diane knows that she is loved, and she is able to give love to her second baby, Sarah.

D. SILENT REFLECTION *(3 minutes)*
Quiet time to get in touch with what moved you most in today's tape.

E. GUIDED JOURNALING *(10 minutes)*
(See page **88**.)

F. COMPANION SHARING *(5 minutes minimum for each person to share)*
Share with your companion what moved you most in today's tape. End by sharing what you are most grateful for and how you need Jesus' help.

G. COMPANION PRAYER *(5 minutes of prayer for each person)*
Pray for your companion for about 5 minutes, either silently or aloud in your own words. Give thanks for what your companion is most grateful for and ask for whatever your companion most needs. Then let your companion pray for you.

H. GROUP SHARING *(15 minutes)*
Share with the whole group what moved you most in today's tape and prayer.

I. Planning For the Future

1. *Optional Sessions*

There are several optional sessions suggested in Appendix E:

Optional Session A:
Simple Ways to Pray
Optional Session B:
In-Depth Prayer for Another
Optional Session C:
Gratitude for Growth Through the Seminar
Optional Session D:
Gratitude for Growth Through Another
Optional Session E:
Eucharist of the Resurrection
for the Deceased
Optional Session F:
Ethnic Potluck

You may wish to conclude the seminar with one or more of these sessions. Take a few minutes to discuss as a group which, if any, of these sessions you wish to use and who will make the arrangements for that session (e.g., renting the film for Optional Session A [see Appendix E], planning a Eucharist for Optional Session E).

2. *After the Seminar Is Over*

Recall your thoughts about the future, as suggested in Home Experience **E** from the previous week's lesson (see page **99**). Have those who are interested in continuing in some way share their suggestions and list them on a blackboard for all to copy. Perhaps there is one thing that the majority would like to do, and the group can take the first steps to implement this. Most likely, there will be several different desires, and those with the same desire might form a small group and discuss how they want to implement their desire. For example, those who want to start new groups for others using the same tapes might plan how they want to work together to share tapes and equipment if they want to start more than one new group. Others might want a weekly Scripture teaching with time to share how they prayed over that Scripture teaching and how it called them to live during the week. See if there are common desires and let implementation groups be formed around them. Let these groups meet for ten minutes to discuss how to implement their desires. Then let the entire group meet together once more so that each of the implementation groups can share their plans for the future. Perhaps others will wish to join them or support them in some way.

J. CLOSING SNACK AND CELEBRATION

An open-ended time to enjoy one another and continue sharing.

II. Home Experiences

A. DAILY HEALING PRAYER *(10 minutes)*

You may wish to use one of the following prayers. Feel free to repeat the same prayer for as many days as you wish, to return to a prayer from a previous lesson, or to pray in some other way.

1. *Prayer For God's Mercy*

- Recall something you have done which you think is hardest for God to forgive.
- Tell Jesus how you feel.
- Recall how Jesus poured his mercy over Diane through Joseph. Let Jesus love and forgive you in the same way.

2. *Contemplation in Action Prayer*

For 10 minutes, do an activity that fosters life, for example:

- gardening
- visiting the elderly
- hugging a child . . . or anyone else who needs a hug
- reading material about a social issue
- writing a letter to a person in prison
- listening to someone who is lonely or depressed.

3. *Embrace Prayer*

(See page **89**.)

B. DAILY JOURNAL *(5 minutes)*

Review your prayer or day and write briefly, sharing with Jesus where you felt the most growth or where you felt the most longing for healing. Then listen as Jesus shares with you how he sees your prayer or day, and write his response. (Perhaps you may wish to share with Jesus how you fostered life today, and let him share with you how he saw you fostering life.)

4. *Preparatory Prayers for Optional Sessions*

Each of the optional sessions invites you to prepare in some way during the preceding week. If your group has decided to meet again for an optional session, consult the Preparatory Homework for that session.

C. OPTIONAL REFLECTION QUESTIONS

*(For group sharing or
personal reflection at home.)*

1. How would you pray for a person like Diane?
2. Why do people choose to abort their babies?
3. Are there any ways in which you place limits on God's mercy?
4. What one thing can you do to foster an environment which gives life and will help a parent choose to give birth to a baby?
5. Can you be against abortion and for euthanasia? for an increase in nuclear arms? for capital punishment?
6. What other pro-life issues are related to abortion (e.g., preventing world hunger, conserving the natural environment, promoting world peace, etc.)? What one thing can you do to foster life?

D. OPTIONAL SUGGESTED READING

Scriptures (See Appendix B, "Scripture Prayer Helps")

Psalm 139: God knows our every thought and action, even while we are in the womb.

Jeremiah 1:4–8: Jeremiah was given his unique identity and call while he was still in the womb.

Matthew 25:31–46: Whatever we do for a person in need, we do for Jesus.

Isaiah 58:6–8: Loving service to the oppressed is the kind of fast that pleases God.

Isaiah 49:15: God cares for the child in the womb even if its own mother forgets it.

Abortion: The Silent Holocaust, by John Powell (Allen, Tex.: Argus, 1981). The author challenges abortion as a violation of our call to love ourselves and one another.

The Psychological Effects of Abortion, edited by David Mall and Walter F. Watts (Washington D.C.: University Publications of America, 1979). See especially "Psychic Causes and Consequences of the Abortion Mentality," by Conrad W. Baars, M.D. Collection of papers presented at a symposium at Loyola University. The findings of this symposium challenge the current majority opinion in the medical community that abortion has little negative psychological after-effect. Dr. Baars' paper discusses abortion as part of a cycle of psychic deprivation and weakness in our culture.

"Aftermath of Abortion: Anniversary Depression and Abdominal Pain," by Jesse O. Cavenar, Allan A. Maltbie and John L. Sullivan, *Bulletin of the Menninger Clinic,* Vol. 42, No. 5, 1978, pp. 433–478. Anniversary depression and abdominal pain are possible after-effects of abortion, apparently "the result of incomplete or abnormal mourning; the person strives to complete the mourning by again unconsciously experiencing the loss."

"Healing of an Abortion Through the Eucharist," by Sheila Fabricant, *Journal of Christian Healing,* Vol. 5, No. 1, Spring 1983, p. 52. Account of a woman who, during a Eucharist for the baby she had aborted twenty years before, experienced the process of giving birth to that child.

"Psychoses Following Therapeutic Abortion," by Jean G. Spaulding and Jesse O. Cavenar, Jr., *American Journal of Psychiatry,* Vol. 135, No. 3, March 1978, pp. 364–365. Two case studies of women who functioned well before an abortion and then experienced psychoses afterward, precipitated by guilt.

"Previous Induced Abortion and Ante-Natal Depression in Primiparae: Preliminary Report of a Survey of Mental Health in Pregnancy," by R. Kumar and Kay Robson, *Psychological Medicine,* Vol. 8, 1978, pp. 711–715. Study of 119 pregnant women which showed a relationship between depression and anxiety during the pregnancy and a previous history of induced abortion. The authors suggest: "Unresolved feelings of grief, guilt and loss may remain dormant long after an abortion until they are apparently reawakened by another pregnancy."

"Postabortive Depressive Reactions in College Women," by Nadia B. Gould, *Journal of the American College Health Association,* Vol. 28, No. 6, June 1980, pp. 316–320. Discusses depression as a frequent post-abortive symptom in college women, and presents this in light of the depression such women may already feel as a result of the tasks of the transition from adolescence to adulthood.

"Emotional Sequelae of Elective Abortion," by Ian Kent, R.C. Greenwood, Janice Loeken and W. Nicholls, *British Columbia Medical Journal,* Vol. 20, No. 4, April 1978, pp. 118–119. Study of fifty women in psychotherapy who had a history of induced abortion. These women had not come for help because of the abortion, and it was only later, after they developed trust relationships with the therapist and therapy group members, that the negative effects of abortion surfaced in the form of mourning, regret, etc. The authors propose that the hurt of abortion is so deep that it surfaces only in a deep trust relationship, and not in the kind of questionnaire surveys that have contributed to current literature claiming there is little negative after-effect from abortion.

Sojourners is a monthly magazine published by a community of people who seek to critique current issues from nuclear weapons to world hunger, all in the light of a biblical perspective. The November 1980 issue was devoted entirely to abortion. Address: 1309 L St. N.W., Washington, D.C. 20005.

Bread for the World has a monthly newsletter which is a valuable resource for pending legislation and analyses of issues as they relate to hunger. Address: 207 E. 16th Ave., New York, N.Y. 10003.

Center for Concern is a group of theologically based economists and other social scientists who publish a monthly newsletter (*Center Focus*) that examines global issues from a Christian perspective. Address: 3700 13th St., N.E., Washington, D.C. 20017.

Amnesty International, 304 W. 58th St., New York, N.Y. 10019, was awarded the 1977 Nobel Prize for Peace. It works on behalf of forgotten and perhaps tortured prisoners by writing letters and putting pressure on authorities.

Common Cause, 2030 M St. N.W., Washington, D.C. 20036, is a non-profit, non-partisan citizens' lobby working to improve the accountability of government members. Presently members are working for greater accountability in campaign financing and accountability in nuclear arms control.

Something Beautiful for God, by Malcolm Muggeridge (New York: Ballantine, 1973). Story of Mother Teresa.

Healing Life's Hurts, by Dennis and Matthew Linn (Ramsey, N.J.: Paulist Press, 1978), Chapter 11, "Fifth Stage: Acceptance." Pages 171–173 of this chapter speak of how inner healing leads to social action.

III. A Note on Limbo

Since the unbaptized could not be saved, Catholic theologians for centuries assigned unbaptized infants the state of Limbo, a state of natural happiness separate from heaven. Today few theologians hold this theory, and the *New Catholic Encyclopedia* concludes, "An official endorsement of limbo's existence by the Church is not to be found." Instead of emphasizing baptism to save infants, the Catholic Church today emphasizes the love of parents who are committed to bringing them into a Christian community. Even when belief in limbo was strong, the Catholic Church recommended trusting the providence of God and invoking the prayer of the Christian community in a Mass of the Angels for deceased babies. Prayers of the Christian community for the deceased child are even more important today with the current emphasis on parents and the Christian community bringing the infant into Jesus' life.

IV. A Note on Spiritism

Spiritism (or spiritualism), the belief that spirits of the dead communicate with the living through a medium, is forbidden by Scripture (Dt 18:10-14; Lv 19:31; 1 Chr 10:13-14). Each of these warnings focuses on a medium calling up the dead to consult the deceased instead of consulting Yahweh. While forbidding even attendance at such séances, the Catholic Church encourages prayer for the deceased.

Prayer for the deceased differs in three ways from the séance's "consulting" that is forbidden in Scripture. First, there is no use of a medium but only of Jesus Christ. Second, there is no person calling up the spirits to be physically present but only Jesus gathering our deceased loved ones wherever he chooses. Third, there is no consulting of the deceased for guidance but rather Jesus inviting the deceased to enter into a more loving relationship with his whole body.

Perhaps the reason so many have discovered spiritism is that so few have discovered the power of the Eucharist where Jesus asks and empowers us and the deceased to love and forgive each other so that we can celebrate the eucharistic meal with him.

APPENDICES

APPENDICES

APPENDIX A

Journaling: writing a love letter

Writing what we want to say to Jesus and what he wants to say to us is a simple form of prayer through journaling. Journaling through writing prayer can help us to grow for two reasons. First, whenever we have an experience and then express it in some tangible way, it becomes more deeply our own. Thus, an inner experience of the Lord's presence becomes more deeply our own when we share it with a friend, paint a picture, dance with joy, sing a psalm of longing for God, or write in a journal.

Second, in writing (as in any other form of creative expression such as art, music or dance), we tap into the intuitive powers of our mind which are the source of spiritual knowledge. Jean Houston, daughter of comedy writer John Houston, tells the story of a time her father took her along with him to deliver a script for the Edgar Bergen/Charlie McCarthy Show. Edgar Bergen was a famous comedian and Charlie McCarthy was his dummy. As Jean and her father neared the open door of Edgar Bergen's hotel room, they heard Edgar Bergen talking to Charlie McCarthy. Jean and her father thought at first that Edgar Bergen was rehearsing, but as they listened to Charlie McCarthy's answers they heard not jokes but statements of profound philosophical and spiritual truth. As they entered the room, John Houston asked Edgar Bergen what he was doing.

"I'm talking to Charlie," Bergen answered. "He's the wisest person I know."

"But Ed, that's you. That's your voice. That's your mind speaking."

"Well, yes, I suppose it is. But you know, when I talk to him and he answers me, I haven't got the faintest idea of what he's going to say . . . and what he says astounds me with its brilliance."

(Quoted from Jean Houston's address to the Annual Convention of the Florida Personnel and Guidance Association, Hollywood, Florida, November 18–20, 1982.)

Like Edgar Bergen, we carry truths within us that we may not even know we know. And as Christians, we have not only the depths of our own spirit within us, but Jesus himself living in us and constantly speaking to us from within. In Christian journaling, done in an atmosphere of prayer, we invite Jesus to use our creative and intuitive powers to tell us his truths about himself, about us and about where he is leading us—truths we may not even know we know.

For years I went to journaling workshops and was sold on the value of journaling to help focus my creative and intuitive powers. But I seldom journaled. When the time for journaling came at the end of the day, I found myself too tired for an exercise that seemed like school homework. Even when I tried to write, little came and I kept reworking its awkward expression. But I also found myself a month or so later wishing I had recorded an insight or moving experience rather than letting it slip away without drawing life from it. I was amazed at how others could talk about what their experiences taught them while I had a hard time even vaguely remembering mine. I only *had experiences* while others were reflecting and *becoming experienced*.

On the other hand, I found I enjoyed writing letters to friends and I would talk about what was happening in my life and what it meant to me. The more I loved a person, the more I had to share myself, and not just *what* was happening but *how I felt* about it. What I could not do in journaling, I was doing in my letters, and finding it not work but fun. For example, I could never journal on what my religious vows meant to me but I wrote four pages to a friend who asked me why I wanted to take final vows. My letter was filled with misspellings and half-thoughts because it was written late at night with my heart more than with my head—and that's why it was so special. After that letter I found new growth in myself: deeper gratitude for and commitment to my Jesuit call, a desire to serve the poor and not just those who are appreciative, a deeper trust in allowing God to work through my poverty, a desire to grow in a celibate love that treats all as my family, and an openness to receive love that made me more grateful for what was given in each moment. I seemed to grow more from writing that one letter than from any other single thing I did that year. I was journaling because I loved a friend so much that I wanted to share my heart, and I focused only on sharing my heart and not on how I spelled or expressed myself.

So I began journaling primarily through my letters, especially Christmas letters sharing the whole year. I could never write my annual Christmas letter until I took time to recall the love of the friend I was writing to, and then I would begin to remember things I wanted to share. I would just recall a good time together, then think about what I most wanted to share—and soon I'd find my pen racing. As I finished the letter, I could even guess how my friend would answer me, because I knew he would say the most loving thing in his heart too. The more I loved another, the more I could also guess at his loving response to me.

Suddenly I found I could do this in prayer with Jesus. I would just relax in his presence and recall a time when I experienced his love—often whatever I was most grateful for that day. Then I would start to write a word of thanks and what I wanted to share with him. It didn't even have to be in sentences because Jesus understands just a word—but sentences did help me to clarify what I really wanted to share. I usually told him what I was feeling and what I most wanted. Then I would write my name, followed by what I thought Jesus would say—just as I could guess what my friend would write because he loves me. It was like prayer, a writing prayer of what I say to Jesus and Jesus says to me.

But is it Jesus or only my imagination replying to me? Any words that help me know more that I am loved are really the voice of Jesus. If I can write a love letter to Jesus it is only because I have heard his voice in the letter he has already written to me. "Love then consists in this, not that we have loved God but that he has first loved us" (1 Jn 4:10). Journaling is simply writing a love letter to Jesus and listening to the love letter he wrote first.

The more my letter is a love letter, the more I will hear anything Jesus says because love makes the heart strain to hear all. Who is the first to hear a baby cry at night? Usually whoever is most concerned about the baby will be sleeping the lightest and will be less likely to turn over for more sleep. A loving mother will hear the baby's cry and also know immediately whether the baby is hungry, wet, tired, afraid, cold or in some danger. Love opens the heart's ears to hear what others ignore and to make sense of what is nonsense to others. The more our love for Jesus is as deep as a mother's love for her baby, the more we will hear the voice of Jesus and understand it.

So, when I question whether it is really Jesus or only my own imagination replying to me, I can ask myself: Do I know more that I am loved and do I have a love for Jesus as deep as a mother's love for her child? The more I can give and receive love with Jesus and others, the more I have heard his voice.

Following are instructions that may help you to journal by writing a love letter to Jesus and receiving the one he writes back to you. But journaling will happen not so much by discovering the best technique as by discovering the best Friend.

INSTRUCTIONS:

1. Share with Jesus by writing in your journal when during this prayer or during the past day you experienced the most struggle or growth.

2. Write in your journal how Jesus responds (what he seems to do or say in response to what you have told him). If you can't get in touch with how Jesus responds, write what most moves you as you speak to him, or what you most *want* him to say to you.

EXAMPLES:

Step 1: Sharing with Jesus

- Focus on Jesus. Relax in his presence—look at a cross or just imagine relaxing with him by a stream or favorite place until you feel quieted and secure.
- With Jesus, look at the day and pray to find the moments of gratitude and of desire for healing.

Gratitude:

The times you are most grateful for, e.g., catching life from a friend, working with care rather than just to get something done, what you did as Jesus rather than alone (e.g., I listened to John as Jesus would but my angry response was me alone), moments of faith or hope, any moment of giving or receiving love with God or another, etc.

Desire for healing:

The times you are not so grateful for, e.g., times of doubt, temptation, gloom, confusion, selfishness, anxiety, running away by working or withdrawing, not listening, failing to choose the present moment with Jesus, any moment of failing to give or receive love with God or another, etc.

Step 2: Writing Jesus' Response

- Focus on Jesus. See the look on his face, hear his words, see the way his hand rests on your shoulder. Get in touch with how he sees all, and ask, "Is His view the same as or different from my view?"
- When you know how Jesus loves you, then write his response to you.

For today, I wrote the following:

Matt, I was happiest today when you listened to John's monologue about his harsh boss and tried to receive love for John and affirm him through your respect. You looked at him and loved him just as I did with the rich young man. But you let some of his anger remain in you and you were restless during your prayer. Maybe you could have just shared with me how you struggle to love a person like John and how you don't like anger in him or in yourself. Let me love you and forgive you the way you are rather than just the way you want to be. Come to me with your burden and I will refresh you.

Journaling Examples from the Movie, "Simple Ways To Pray"

In our movie, "Simple Ways to Pray," seven people each took five minutes to go through the same two steps of sharing with Jesus and then being attentive to Jesus' response. Following are three examples from this lesson of what a person shared with Jesus and then what their journal entry might be. (*Note:* For using the film or videotape "Simple Ways to Pray" as an optional session, see Appendix D. To order, see Appendix E.)

Example 1: A journal entry recording what Jesus says.
(After sharing with Jesus four things about his job and family situation that he wished would change, Chuck wrote down what he thought Jesus was saying to him.)
"I know the hurts you feel. Men have hurt me too. Trust in me and have faith and I will help you."
Thus, one way to journal is to write down in a few sentences, as Chuck did, just what you sense Jesus wants to say to you.

Example 2: A journal entry recording what Jesus does.
(After sharing with Jesus what she wished she could have said or done for her son Scott before he died, Tommy watches in her spirit and describes what Jesus does.)
"Jesus is sitting on the bed with Scott. He has his hand on Scott's head. Then he puts his arm around Scott's shoulder."
Thus, a second way to journal would be to write in a few sentences what Jesus wants to do for you or another.

Example 3: A journal entry recording what moves you the most as you speak to Jesus, or what you most want him to say or do.
(After silently sharing with Jesus how sorry she is that on the day she wanted to run away from her father he had a heart attack and died, Gale begins to cry and writes the following.)
"I want to know that he (my father) loves me. Most of all, I want him to know how much I love him. I never told him that, Lord."
The third way to journal is to write in a few sentences what moved you the most, i.e., what you most wanted or experienced most intensely.

Additional Suggestions for Journaling

If you don't have a sense of what Jesus is saying to you, perhaps one of the following will help.

1. Look at a picture of Jesus looking at you. Look at him with love until you sense what he wants to say, just as a mother's love knows what the wordless face of her baby is saying.

2. Ask Jesus when he felt like you or when he met someone like you. Today are you more bold than Peter or doubting Thomas, Martha or Mary, the prodigal son or the elder brother, the Pharisee or the publican, or . . .?

3. With Jesus' love in your heart, what would you tell your friend if he or she wrote what you have written in your journal? Write this response to your friend.

4. Try reading your journal entry aloud, listening to it with love and understanding. Then write your response.

5. Simply write what you most want Jesus to say to you, and then underline the parts that would come from a God who is perfect Love and Truth.

APPENDIX B

Scripture prayer helps

The following steps are only a guide and should be set aside when you find your own way to meet Jesus in the Scriptures.

1. *Passage*. Choose a Scripture passage you want to pray rather than have to pray. Begin by asking, "What do I want?" Maybe you are tired and want to rest with Jesus on the lakeshore (John 21), or maybe you are fearful and need courage to walk on water (Matthew 14:22–33). Maybe you need to forgive a stinging remark with Jesus on the cross (Luke 23:34). If you have no strong desires, you might return to the passage you read most recently that spoke to your heart. Ask Jesus in your own words for what you want.

2. *Read*. Treat the passage as you would a personal letter from the person who loves you the most. Read the passage in a reverent whisper, so that each word is spoken directly to you with the power that made Levi leave everything for the sake of just two words, "Follow me." Read the passage three times: once for understanding with your mind, once to love Jesus and once to be loved by Jesus.

3. *Focus on Jesus*. Close your eyes and take a few minutes to quiet your body in a relaxed yet erect listening posture. Then begin to breathe in and out the word, "Jesus," building up a hunger for him as you hunger for breath. When you breathe out, give Jesus yourself and all your tensions, while hearing him say your name in the way he alone loves you and calls you. How you continue to say "Jesus" changes because with each breath you can open a deeper part of yourself to Jesus and give him a deeper part of your life. If you get distracted, simply return to saying, "Jesus." Continue to do this until you sense how Jesus is looking at you and loves you.

4. *Enter the scene*. Enter whatever part of the scene in the passage moved you the most. Once you are with Jesus, you might use your senses to get more fully into the scene. You might walk with Jesus down the dusty Emmaus road, adapting your gait to his and listening as he reveals how he sees what is discouraging you. You might smell the dust and the perfumed lilies of the field, feel the warm sunlight and uneven stones under your feet, hear the birds chirp to punctuate your steps, and search Jesus' face to guess what he is going to say. It's easy to guess because Jesus (Love Itself) always says only the most loving possible words. When you get in touch with what you most need to hear, you are hearing Jesus calling you to deeper faith, hope, love, surrender and openness.

5. *Pause*. Once you are with Jesus, enjoy him as you would your best friend. Revel in loving and being loved, in surrendering all, and in knowing his mind and heart so well that you can guess his reactions. What does he do or say that surprises you, challenges you or strengthens you? How does he respond to your needs? What does he want? If you feel lost, return to the passage and then to Jesus again. Don't worry about having the "right" images or about how you are praying. Just rest with Jesus, surrendering all and taking him into your heart.

6. *Thanks*. End by sharing your heart and giving thanks for all that has happened. Open yourself to be grateful even for the difficult, distraction-filled, dry times that deepen your love and make you want to give even when there is little response. These times can make you aware of how much your prayer and entire life depend on Jesus rather than on your own efforts. Ask Jesus to reveal any way in which you may be able to improve your prayer and ask him for a hunger for the Giver and not just for the gift.

APPENDIX C

Tasks of the group leader

If a group intends to go through the seminar together, a leader should be chosen who can either delegate or be responsible for the following tasks:

I. BEFORE THE MEETING

Listen to the first four sessions long before the first meeting. If there are any defects in the tape, do not hesitate to return the tape and ask for a replacement. Repeat this process with each additional tape. Pay special attention to the fourth session's format requiring more leadership. Plan the timing and format variations that will best meet the group's needs (e.g., companion sharing in fours for variety).

II. DURING THE MEETING

- Initiate the Common Opening Prayer and Songs.
- Do the timing for: Silent Reflection, Companion Sharing, Companion Prayer and Group Sharing. Be sure to signal when Companion Prayer starts lest participants spend all their time continuing to share.
- Lead any other group experiences (Guided Journaling, Group Sharing). Be sensitive to giving all a chance to share.
- If you are going to use an optional session (cf. Appendix D), help the group decide what material will be covered during the next meeting. Take responsibility for the necessary arrangements for that meeting (e.g., procuring a Mass celebrant, film "Simple Ways To Pray," etc.).
- Enlist volunteers to help with the closing snack and celebration. (You might want to use this time to celebrate birthdays and anniversaries of group members.)
- At the end of the seminar, facilitate deciding if and how to continue meeting after the seminar ends. Help implement these decisions.

III. PASTORAL CARE

The group leader is also entrusted with a pastoral concern for the participants. Even though this seminar focuses on praying with another, participants will discover areas in themselves needing healing. Almost all the dynamic of healing will happen as the leader encourages the group to listen with empathy and love, and to pray rather than give advice. However, if some participants need help beyond what they are receiving with their companion(s), it is helpful to have other persons available who can listen and provide this extra help. In other cases, the role of the group leader may be to find someone else who can help. Occasionally, it may be necessary to recommend professional help.

The most important part of pastoral concern is to pray intercessory prayer daily, if possible, asking that each participant meet Jesus through his or her prayer and through the process of sharing with a companion(s).

Optional Session B:
In-Depth Prayer for Another

Preparatory Homework
Any of the Daily Healing Prayers suggested for Lesson 6.

Group Meeting

I. COMMON OPENING PRAYER
(5 minutes)

PRAYER FOR ANOTHER
1. With your companion, get in a group of four people.

2. Choose one person who would like prayer, and pray for this person in whatever way the Lord moves you for the next 10–45 minutes. The Lord will not move you to pray for a person in a way that violates that person, so begin by finding out how that person would like to receive prayer.

3. Spend 10 minutes or more sharing with one another what you experienced during the prayer. For example, what touched you most? What was distracting? What was helpful? What was not so helpful?

GROUP SHARING
Use your remaining time to share with the entire group your experience of praying for another.

CLOSING SNACK AND CELEBRATION
An open-ended time to enjoy each other and continue sharing.

Optional Session C:
Gratitude for Growth
Through the Seminar

Preparatory Homework
Ask Jesus to review the past weeks with you and show you the moments that please him most. Finally, choose a moment or event from the past eight (or twelve) weeks that summarizes what has touched you or most changed your life.

II. Group Experience

A. COMMON OPENING PRAYER (5 minutes)

B. DESCRIPTION OF THE SESSION
The leader of the group might take a few minutes to describe the plans for this session.

C. SCRIPTURE READING
(Use one of the following, or another appropriate passage).

Matthew 5:14–16
You are the light of the world. (Perhaps read it in a darkened room and have each person light a candle later, during the sharing time.)

Mark 6:34–44
Parable of the loaves multiplied through the disciples' hands. (Perhaps give each person a piece of bread and let each one get in touch with how the Lord has given him or her gifts to share with others during the past weeks. As each shares about this growth during the sharing time, let each also share the bread.)

Matthew 13:4–12 or 13:31–32
Parables of the seed. (Perhaps give each person a seed and let each one get in touch with what the Lord has given each to plant. Then let each one plant it during the sharing time, perhaps in a pot of soil.)

Matthew 25:14–30
Parable of the silver pieces. (Perhaps give each person a blank check on which to write what each has been given and is returning to the Lord.)

Luke 21:1–4
Widow's mite. (Perhaps give each person a penny and let each get in touch with how, although the gift each can give may not seem like much, the Lord looks only at the generosity behind it.)

D. SHARING
1. Option I:
- Divide into groups of 4 to 6, including your companion(s).
- Silence. Take a few minutes to let the Scripture sink in. Let each person ask Jesus what gift or growth (symbolized by the light, bread, seed, silver piece or mite) he has given during the past weeks to me and to each person in my group, so that we can give thanks and bless the growth. Since we are all Christ's body and share all of his gifts, let us ask Jesus to reveal all our gifts and help us to be as excited about another's gift as we are about our own gift.

APPENDIX D

Optional sessions

Optional Session A:
Simple Ways to Pray

(This session is for those who have not taken the *Prayer Course for Healing Life's Hurts*. "Simple Ways To Pray" is the first lesson of the *Prayer Course*. See Appendix E for information on purchase or rental of the film or video tape "Simple Ways to Pray.")

I. Preparatory Homework

Any of the Daily Healing Prayers suggested for Lesson 6.

II. Group Meeting

A. COMMON OPENING PRAYER *(5 minutes)*

B. VIDEO TAPE OR MOVIE:
"Simple Ways To Pray" (30 minutes)

The power to heal is the power to love. There are as many ways of praying as there are ways of loving.

1. Praying through our breathing, emptying our darkness as we exhale and inhaling Jesus' love until we are able to breathe out his love to the Father (e.g., woman filled with fear).

2. Silent prayer by three people: one who is suffering in the same way, one who has been healed of that illness and the one who loves the person the most (e.g., woman with back pain).

3. Becoming another and letting ourselves be loved by the Father as that person (e.g., Leo and his father, Frank).

4. Recalling a painful memory and inviting Jesus into it: the prayer of creative imagination (e.g., Tommy and her son, Scott).

5. Filling another with the Lord's love and letting tears be a prayer (e.g., woman praying for her father).

6. Writing how we feel and listening [to re]sponse (e.g., man who wrote out his hur[t]).

7. Praying for someone we love by [placing him] or her into the Father's hands (e.g., wom[an and] her husband, Denny).

8. Praying for another by looking a[t them and] seeing them through Jesus' eyes and [saying a] prayer for them (e.g., woman praying for [ ]).

C. SILENT REFLECTION *(3 minutes)*

Quiet time to get in touch with wh[at touched us] most in today's tape.

D. GUIDED JOURNALING *(10 min[utes])*
(See pages **88.**)

E. COMPANION SHARING *(5 minu[tes]*
for each person to share)

Share with your companion wha[t touched us] most in "Simple Ways To Pray." End by [saying what] you are most grateful for and how you ne[ed]

F. COMPANION PRAYER *(5 minutes*
for each person)

Pray for your companion for about [ ] ther silently or aloud in your own word[s] for what your companion is most grate[ful for and] for whatever your companion most ne[eds. Let] your companion pray for you.

G. GROUP SHARING *(15 minutes)*

Share with the whole group what m[ost touched us] in "Simple Ways To Pray."

H. CLOSING SNACK AND CELEBR[ATION]

An open-ended time to enjoy one [another and] continue sharing.

- Let any one person begin by mentioning another in the group and describing how he or she has seen Jesus in that person and how the person has helped him or her to grow. Thank Jesus for these things. Let each of the others in the small group do the same to affirm and give thanks for this person.
- After all in the group have described and given thanks for how they see Jesus in the person, let that person respond by describing and thanking the Lord for his or her own growth and for how the group has nurtured this growth.
- End by having the whole group pray over this person to bless these gifts and growth. (This is the time to light the candle, share the bread, plant the seed, give the check or penny to the Lord.)
- Repeat the last three steps with each person in the group.

2. Option II:

- The entire group remains together.
- Silence. Take a few minutes to let the Scripture sink in. Let each person ask Jesus what gift or growth (symbolized by the light, bread, seed, silver piece or mite) he has given during the past 8 (or 12) weeks to me and to each person in my group, so that we can give thanks and bless the growth. Since we are all Christ's body and share all of his gifts, let us ask Jesus to reveal all our gifts and help us to be as excited about another's gift as we are about our own gift.
- Those who wish to might share their moment of greatest growth during the preceding weeks.
- After each person who wishes to do so has shared his or her moment of greatest growth, the rest of the group might want to pray over that person to bless the gifts and growth they have described. (This is the time to light the candle, share the bread, plant the seed, give the check or penny to the Lord.)

E. SILENT PRAYER

The session might conclude with 5 minutes of silence, with all present holding hands in a circle and letting Jesus' love pass from one to another.

Optional Session D: Gratitude for Growth Through Another

I. Preparatory Homework

Choose a person from your group. Ask Jesus to show you how that person has given you life (e.g., that person's smile, ability to struggle, gift of listening, spirit of celebration, etc.). Do this exercise with each person in your group.

II. Group Experience

A. COMMON OPENING PRAYER *(5 minutes)*

B. SHARING YOUR GRATITUDE

Get into twos. Share with each other for a few minutes how you have given each other life. When you have finished, move on to any other person in the room who is free.

C. CLOSING SNACK AND CELEBRATION

An open-ended time to enjoy one another and continue sharing.

Optional Session E: Eucharist of the Resurrection for the Deceased

(Ideally the theme of praying for the deceased should include a group Mass of the Resurrection. If a group Mass cannot be arranged, you may ask your parish priest to offer a Mass for your deceased loved ones and then attend that Mass. Or you can also pray for the deceased at any Mass you attend.)

Christian tradition points to the Eucharist as a powerful way to pray for the deceased. During the first century Christians hiding in the catacombs offered the Eucharist on the tombs of their martyrs and especially on anniversaries prayed for the dead entombed around them. By the third century it was customary to pray for the dead on the 7th, 9th, 13th and 40th days after a person's death. By this time special prayers for the dead were included in every Mass, as reflected in the third century Canon of Hippolytus. In the following centuries stories circulated of how at Eucharist Sts. Perpetua, Malachy, Thomas Aquinas, Teresa of Avila and others helped the souls in purgatory. This developed into widespread devotion to these souls and the celebration of All Souls' Day. Unfortunately, belief in the power of the Eucharist to help the souls in purgatory degenerated into a set number of hurried Masses promising sure results. This magical emphasis on numbers and formulas was rightly rejected by the Reformers, but they also overreacted by rejecting all prayer for the dead. Today many groups, such as the Anglicans, are rediscovering the need to pray for the dead, especially at Eucharist.

The Eucharist, where Jesus' blood is offered to forgive and heal all generations, is the main way the Council of Trent suggested that Roman Catholics can help the deceased. Today many are discovering how the Eucharist offered for the deceased also heals the living as they come into a deeper relationship with Jesus and the deceased. Dr. Kenneth McAll has over one thousand cases of emotional or physical healing occurring with his clients primarily through a Eucharist offered for the deceased. (*Healing the Family Tree*, by Dr. Kenneth McAll, London: Sheldon Press, 1982).

For whom should you pray? Seven questions may help.

1. Whom do I miss most in my family? Am I tied too much to that person?
2. Who were the most unloved and difficult people in my family? Who hurt me?
3. Who died without a sense of being loved (e.g., suicides, accidents, painful deaths, etc.)?
4. Has anyone in the family been involved in the occult?
5. Have there been any stillbirths, abortions or miscarriages—children who need to be lovingly committed to God?
6. Are there any ancestors who have handed down destructive patterns?
7. Did these questions bring to mind any person outside my family tree who may need prayer?

It is helpful to write down the names of the deceased needing prayer and then underline the one person you will focus on during the Mass. If possible, begin by placing the list on the altar (if it is a special Mass for the dead) or hold the paper in your hand throughout an ordinary Mass.

You can join Jesus in loving and forgiving the deceased by the following:

Penance Rite: Ask forgiveness for any ways you and others hurt that deceased person. Then with Jesus forgive that person for the ways you and others may have been hurt by him or her. Ask Jesus to show you how he wants to ask his Father to heal and love the deceased person during this Eucharist.

Offertory: Offer the deceased person to the Father and thank the Father for all the good that has come to you and others because of the deceased person. Let the Father bless all the good in that person and all the ways that goodness has been shared with others.

Canon: Let Jesus standing before the Father raise the deceased person to the Father just as he did at his death. Lovingly pray for the deceased person at the prayer for the departed.

Communion: Receive Communion and then ask Jesus to fill you with his precious blood, healing all the hurts, sinful patterns or occult bondage that may block the fullness of his life in you. Then ask Jesus to let his blood wash away everything negative you have inherited and to strengthen all your positive inheritance. Breathe in "Jesus" and breathe out anything negative (fear, anger, negative thoughts, patterns of sin, etc.) until you have no more darkness to breathe out and you are also exhaling the life of Jesus. When you are ready to give life as Jesus, then see his precious blood flow from you to the deceased person, healing all his or her hurts, sinful patterns and occult weakness. Do the same for the deceased on your father's and mother's sides of the family. Don't try to remember everyone, but let Jesus show you which ones most need his life and how he prays for each. If you don't sense Jesus' prayer for a person, just say "Jesus" silently, exhaling his life into that deceased person.

Blessing: Ask that you and the deceased might come closer to Jesus, thereby blessing each other.

If you sense that some deceased persons still need more life, you can pray for them during the day or at the next Eucharist you attend, as did St. Malachy:

St. Bernard's Account of St. Malachy

The sister of this saint (Malachy) was so worldly-minded that her brother determined not to see her anymore as long as she lived. But although he did not see her in the flesh, he was to see her again in the spirit. After her death, one night he heard a voice telling him that his sister was at the door, complaining that she had had nothing to eat for thirty days. The saint, when he awoke, forthwith understood what food it was of which she was in need, for it was exactly thirty days since he had offered the Sacrifice of the living bread for her. He now again began to give her this benefit, which he had withheld from her. Soon he saw her coming up to the church. But she could not yet enter, as she was still wearing a black garment. He continued to offer the Holy Sacrifice for her every day, and soon saw her a second time, dressed in a lighter garment. Finally, he saw her a third time, clad entirely in white, and surrounded by blessed spirits.

Optional Session F: Ethnic Potluck

In gratitude for what God has done through your heritage and for how God has blessed you through one another, you may wish to celebrate with an ethnic potluck. Each person can bring a dish that represents his or her ethnic heritage. Some may also wish to wear ethnic clothing. Before the meal, you may wish to share the special meanings of the ethnic food you brought or perhaps of the clothes you are wearing. You may even wish to share with each other what positive characteristics, traits or attributes have been handed down to you through your father's ancestry and your mother's ancestry. Share why you are proud of your ancestry. For example:

> Irish ancestry—humor
> German ancestry—hard work
> Polish ancestry—perseverance
> Spanish ancestry—celebration
> Jewish ancestry—study

Then enjoy each other's ethnic food and celebrate how you have blessed one another during the seminar.

APPENDIX E

Where to order tapes and films

A. Tapes

1. *Praying with Another for Healing*, by Dennis and Matthew Linn and Sheila Fabricant. Twelve 30-minute sessions on video or audio tape, plus course manual.

2. *Prayer Course for Healing Life's Hurts*, by Dennis and Matthew Linn and Sheila Fabricant. Twenty-four 30-minute sessions on video or audio tape, plus course manual.

3. *Dying To Live: Spiritual Care for the Dying and Their Families*, by Bill and Jean Carr and Dennis and Matthew Linn. Eight 30-minute sessions on video or audio tape. This series can be ordered with the book upon which it is based, *Healing the Dying*, by Mary Jane Linn, Dennis Linn and Matthew Linn.

Purchase

(above tapes and books)
Paulist Press
545 Island Rd.
Ramsey, N.J. 07446
(201) 825-7300

Rental

(above videotapes in VHS only)
Video Rentals
4453 McPherson
St. Louis, Mo. 63108
(314) 533-8423

B. Film

"Simple Ways to Pray," 30-minute, 16mm. film by Dennis & Matthew Linn. (Also available in videotape form from Paulist Press, as the first session of the *Prayer Course* listed above.)
Purchase or Rental of Film
Mass Media Ministries
2116 N. Charles St.
Baltimore, Md. 21218
(301) 727-3720

C. Other Resources

1. A wide variety of audio tapes on prayer, healing and related topics by Matt and Dennis Linn, Richard Rohr and other speakers is available from:
ALU
504 Antioch Ln.
Ballwin, Mo. 63011

2. The School for Spiritual Growth and Inner Healing, by Fr. Jim Wheeler, S.J., is a two-year home study program focused on healing through scriptural prayer. For information, write:
School for Spiritual Growth
and Inner Healing
4204 San Ysidro Ave.
Albuquerque, N.M. 87107